Tools in the Learning Trade

A Guide to Eight Indispensable Tools for College Students

by Barbara Currier Bell

with a contribution by Winifred A. Asprey

The Scarecrow Press, Inc.
Metuchen, N.J., & London
1984

Library of Congress Cataloging in Publication Data

Bell, Barbara Currier, 1941-
  Tools in the learning trade.

  Includes index.
    1. Reference books. 2. College students—Books and
reading. 3. Study, Method of. I. Title.
Z711.B43   1984   011'.02   83-15105
ISBN 0-8108-1655-5

To my students
and to learners everywhere

CONTENTS

ACKNOWLEDGMENTS

EVEN A SMALL BOOK like this one builds up debts. I am grateful to the Columbia, Wesleyan, and Fairfield University libraries and librarians for both access and assistance. Harry Shaw, who has spent more than my lifetime dealing with the subject of writing and books about writing, gave supportive advice. The editors of *College Composition and Communication*, *College English* (journals sponsored by the National Council of Teachers of English), *Scholarly Publishing*, and *The New York Times* Education section helped by publishing certain portions or versions of the material presented here. Local bookstore personnel tolerated visits both numerous and lengthy. Many reviews, bibliographies and other scholarly works even beyond those mentioned in Appendix I were informative. Students, colleagues and friends made contributions. My husband, Donald C. Bell, turned photographer for the illustrations. Linda Galasso rendered crabbed drafts into clean type, and Alice Burton and my family gave me the time.

Finally, come you, the users of *Tools in the Learning Trade*. A guide covering as many items as this one does, especially considering the frequency of their revision and the importance of their use, invites active participation from those who read it. Recognize that you are involving yourself in a process. Once you have a copy of this guide for your own, mark up its pages, make notes on your favorite tools, and whatever comments, corrections, or updates you may have, thank you in advance for contributing them. Learning thrives on a spirit of collaboration.

BARBARA CURRIER BELL

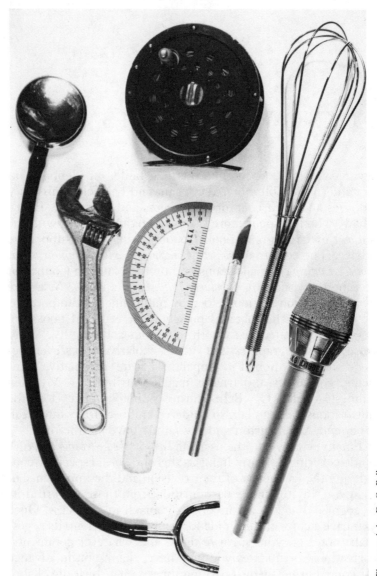

Photograph by D. C. Bell.

INTRODUCTION

> *In a time not so long ago when one craftsman was largely responsible for building an entire home, several master carpenters presented their toolchests to a prospective client. He inspected their tools: the newness of the edges and the wear of the handles, the art of wood-joining in the chests, the strength of the joints, the cleverness of construction. The client chose a carpenter by the condition of his tools; it told him something about the way tools and craftsman worked together.*
>
> Toolchest

If you are a learner, just like a person working at any other trade, you need tools. In fact, the quickest way to succeed is to get the best set of tools available and master their use. Some of the tools are mechanical, such as a ballpoint pen, a reading lamp, and a typewriter. The tools you need to take you as far as you want to go, however, are the ones that provide information—reference tools.

This is a guide to eight indispensable reference tools for you to own if you wish to master the learning trade. Reference tools are not easy to evaluate or use without assistance. In recent years they have grown enormously. If you tried to buy one lately, you probably have felt both surprise and confusion. You may assume a professor can give you some advice, for as one official of a college teachers' organization stated, "College students tend to buy [the reference tools] their instructors tell them to buy." But many times professors go no further than deciding course texts. They may want to encour-

age your independence, or they may not be able to keep up with the latest reference tools, especially in fields not their own; in general, most of them are not used to thinking in terms of a reference "kit" at all.

A librarian's guide to reference sources will not tell you what you need to know, either. These guides are not meant to be selective. They are short on advice about which types of tools are most important, and about which title to choose within a type; most either assume or ignore too much about your ability to handle the tool.

Finally, you will not find guidance in any of those books on the market with titles such as *The How to Go to College Book*, *A Student's Survival Manual*, even, *How to Study*. They tell you how to get along with your roommate, how to take notes, how to pay for your phone bill, and where to eat, but they never tell you what learning tools to buy.

The eight tools discussed in this book are unconventional. A couple are not even books. They are meant to help you with the widest possible range of learning tasks. A rough selection was made initially according to the appropriateness of tools for learning at the advanced high school or college level on up, and the frequency with which they are recommended by other sources. That list was refined to arrive at specific choices for comparison. If you like, you can think of the recommendations made at the end of this sifting as the minimum number of important tools you need when you have a learning job to do and the library is closed, your professor is not available, and your friend in the class is away for the weekend.

In each section of "The Eight Tools," pointers about using a particular type of tool are given, and these turn into criteria for evaluating titles within that type. Here, the reasons for choosing a tool are more important than the ratings, not only because reasons are more interesting, but also because they do not go out of date as fast, and because, as has been said, not all titles within each type could be covered. Each section concludes with a list of ten sample questions that can be referred to the tool discussed. The specific questions listed are not meant to be typical; rather, each illustrates a *type* of question that students often ask. You can use these to compare with specific questions of your own, to clarify the more general

points about how each tool should be used, or, in some cases, to help you "test" tools for yourself.

The chapter "Investing in Yourself" addresses some concerns you may have about what the tools cost. The Conclusion and the two appendices are designed to further explain the materials. They route you toward supply houses of learning tools and give you advice about choosing once you have become familiar with the essentials. Appendix I also supplies notes on the epigraphs or other quotations that appear in the text.

"Learning is in a bad state," critics of America's educational system have been saying, or lately shouting. Among other remedies, "Back to basics" has been the remedial cry. What can be more basic than good tools? Once you have gotten your tools, rig up a place for them near you and use them as frequently as effective learning deserves. After all, according to the epigraph at the beginning, "By thy tools shall ye be known."

The Eight Tools

"You Can't Get There on a Flat Tire." Courtesy of Student Publication Service, Evanston, Ill.

1. DICTIONARIES

Neither is a dictionary a bad book to read . . . it is full of suggestion,—the raw material of possible poems and histories.

Ralph Waldo Emerson (1803–1882)

First, you will need a general dictionary. No doubt you already have one. But it may be the one you used in eighth grade, or an old one from your family's den, or a small paperback version, and none of these is good enough. Which one is? Dictionaries are as thick as graffiti on dormitory walls, but choosing among them often amounts to a guess or a glance at the price tag. Perhaps some vague memory of someone else's opinion also affects the choice. Most likely, though, you could use some more constructive criteria. Those below are aimed at helping you choose, as well as at helping you get the most out of your dictionary. The main principle to keep in mind is that language is not simple; it is a resource that can be mined for rich rewards.

SCOPE

A collegiate dictionary (or semi-unabridged), with 130,000–170,000 entries, will be a better buy than the various kinds of abridged dictionaries (known as "desk," "concise," "compact," or "pocket"), having below 55,000 entries. It is also better than the other extreme, an unabridged dictionary. De-

spite what you may fear while preparing for an SAT test, studies have shown that educated people seldom need more than 50,000 words for "taking care of business," and while college students should have access to more than that number (considering the heavy language demands placed on them) they do not need over 250,000. Playing the numbers game with dictionaries is almost valueless beyond these rough groupings.

The types of words covered should include scientific or technological vocabulary, so-called "literary" vocabulary, and colloquial vocabulary. Do not trust advertisements on this score. Try a test list of words yourself.

AUTHORITY

Only a company experienced in dictionary-making can afford the large capital investment, knowledgeable staff, and extensive, current word-file for a publishing effort as huge and complex as a dictionary. The five publishing houses represented in the list of collegiate dictionaries in this chapter are highly regarded. Dictionaries put out by other publishing companies need to be carefully checked. Note particularly that the name "Webster's" may appear in the title of dictionaries published by several different companies, and does not by itself indicate authority.

TIMELINESS

While updated editions of many dictionaries are constantly being published (which is why no dates are given in the list below), thorough revisions are made every 10–15 years at most. By the time a new edition of your dictionary comes out, the general learning demands on your vocabulary will have diminished, and you will have discovered a specialized dictionary for use in a new trade. So keep your old dictionary, and if you like, just buy a new one for your more specific needs.

TREATMENT OF VOCABULARY

Many learners feel about definitions the way slaves do about their masters: they obey mechanically and with hatred. Liberate yourself. Start by ignoring the ads for dictionaries as "instant words" or "answer books." Words are more than the definitions you can write down on cue cards and good dictionaries enrich your appreciation for meaning by adding "context" information about synonyms and antonyms, grammar, usage, and etymology to routine instructions on spelling, pronunciation, and syllabication. If you use a dictionary merely as a source from which to copy, it is not a tool in your control. Use it, instead, to help you think.

ENCYCLOPEDIC FEATURES

Dictionaries have come to include all sorts of tables, charts, historical and geographical data, college directories, and other types of information. Do not settle for all this at the expense of word entries, and do not invest in the encyclopedic supplements that some dictionary publishers offer. Save your money for a one-volume general encyclopedia, as recommended in a later section. Names and places should be listed in the dictionary's main text. Other types of information are generally in appendices, where they are easier to find.

BIAS

In recent years, women and racial minority groups have spotlighted the sexist and racist social attitudes that language often conveys. Dictionaries have been viewed as accomplices in discrimination. You should be alert to this problem and try to select a dictionary that does not unconsciously support stereotypes or ignore words that have been added to the language to correct these shortcomings.

The five most commonly recommended collegiate dictionaries are:

American Heritage Dictionary, new college edition
Funk & Wagnalls Standard College Dictionary
The Random House College Dictionary, revised edition
Webster's New Collegiate Dictionary, 8th edition
Webster's New World Dictionary, 2nd college edition

Besides having about the same number of words and costing, weighing, and measuring about the same, these dictionaries are authoritative, stay as current as possible, make about equal efforts with vocabulary coverage and treatment, and contain roughly the same amount of encyclopedic material. They have all made efforts to improve on the score of bias.

Despite these similarities, some comparisons among the dictionaries are instructive. Here are five criteria for evaluating a collegiate dictionary, in addition to the general ones mentioned earlier.

1. *Design.* This is one aspect of a dictionary not usually given top billing, but it is crucial. For instance, you should look at the pictures. They are not just decorative. To find out what that legendary creature the "manticore" is, or to understand a "penumbra," you would be better off with a drawing than with a written description. Of course, most collegiate dictionaries have illustrations—600–1500 on the average—but besides variations in number, there are variations in the way pictures are displayed. Also, you should insist on comfortable reading: The text should not be cramped; pages should have generous margins; guide words should be efficient; type size in general should be large enough, and the type size or face should be varied to aid in distinguishing parts of definitions.

2. *Clarity of Definition.* Clarity matters more than most other aspects of definition for a learner because so often the word you have to look up is abstract or general. If you find "freedom" defined as "liberty" and "liberty" defined as a characteristic of "democracy" and so forth, you are going around in circles with abstractions. Language becomes especially frustrating at this level. One aid to clarity is the use of examples. Not all dictionaries offer "real" examples (quotations from

published sources) as opposed to hypothetical ones (staff-written phrases). The real examples are always more lively and often more instructive.

3. *Etymology.* The histories of words record essential dimensions of meaning. "Villain," for instance, comes from the Latin word for farm, so originally villains simply were farm laborers. The word's present meaning of "evildoer" includes the sense of a villain's being morally apart from most people. The word's history is what provides that sense, subtly incorporating a long-established stereotype about the lower-class origins of crime. As another example, teachers are fond of saying that "educate" comes from the Latin word meaning "to lead, draw or bring out," but did you know that "learning" goes back to a much earlier word meaning "rut"? Etymologies allow you to appreciate the organic quality of words, the way each one takes on a life of its own, and the extent to which that life is linked with others.

4. *Usage Level.* Usage labels indicate certain restrictions on the uses of words. For example, a word may be used only in the West (dogie), or it may have become obsolete (fustian), or it may be used in some specialized field (*habeas corpus*). Labels marking these sorts of peculiarities are not controversial and most dictionaries agree on them. Labels regarding usage *level*—indicating whether a word is slang, obscene, colloquial, or suited for formal use—are *not* so commonly agreed upon and touch off concern about "good" and "bad" language. Those who prefer a prescriptive approach either want to see only "good" words in the dictionary, or, if all sorts are included, to have usage level stressed. ("A dictionary and grammar may stay our speech in a perfect use forever," said one sixteenth-century scholar.) Those on the descriptive side want to include as many words as possible and to play down usage level. ("Language is the work of man, of a being from whom permanence and stability cannot be derived," said Dr. Samuel Johnson, 18th-century author of one of the earliest and greatest English dictionaries.) Learners, however, need both inclusiveness and a stress on usage level, because their business is not to affect language behavior in one way or another but rather to explore what is known about usage as a particularly rich feature of language.

5. *Front Matter.* This can make or break you in your use of

the dictionary as a learning tool. It is the instruction manual, telling you how the dictionary is put together. It also includes articles on the history of the English language, on the structure of languages in general and ours in particular, and on language usage in our culture. These are written by experts, but not for experts. Some of them are masterpieces of condensation. They are thorough and well-balanced. The information they provide, the challenges they pose, and the perspective they convey offer as much of an education as you might hope to glean from several English classes; yet this material costs nothing extra and can be read in one sitting. To read it is to grasp the ways that language has made human beings thrive.

With these five criteria in mind, you can look at the main collegiate dictionaries more closely. They are discussed in alphabetical order.

American Heritage is the newest. Its design makes it especially easy to use. It has the most spacious format of the five, a type design that aids discrimination, and many more illustrations than its competitors. In addition, the illustrations are placed more prominently and attractively. Its definitions are sometimes not as clear as those of its competitors, but it balances that deficiency with probably the largest number of illustrative quotations and staff-written examples. It stresses etymology the most, making the greatest effort to carry words back to roots in Indo-European (a hypothetical "Adam or Eve" for Western languages), even appending a table of those roots. Also, its etymologies are easier to understand, because it does not abbreviate the names of parent languages. Finally, it has more prefatory essays than its rivals and covers more ground in them.

The Second College Edition of *American Heritage* updates the New College Edition and is more recent than any of its rivals. It has not yet made its way onto the lists in the usual sources of recommendation, but in certain ways it is less useful for learners than its predecessor. Its design is generally less spacious, and it has fewer illustrations, although still substantially more than the others. The table of Indo-European roots has been eliminated and front matter is shorter and less diversified. While many new words and definitions have been add-

ed, with old ones cut or revised, and while in other general ways *American Heritage*'s character is intact, the earlier edition remains more accommodating.

Funk & Wagnalls has the greatest number of illustrations after *American Heritage* and the largest type size of any of the dictionaries reviewed here, so its design is a plus. It draws on a larger unabridged dictionary, the *Funk & Wagnalls Standard* (with particularly well-respected scholars in charge), in striving for simplicity, however, its definitions become too brief. Etymologies are not extensively pursued. With regard to usage level, it offers more than at least one competitor but it does not pay much attention to prefatory material.

Random House falls in the middle as to design. It sets a basic standard in its definitions, etymologies, and usage level labels. Based on an excellent, though relatively small, unabridged dictionary, but unable to offer the amount of encyclopedic material that makes its parent unique, the collegiate *Random House* suffers by comparison. Its front matter is thorough, but does not try to move into new territory.

Webster's New Collegiate—"the" *Webster's*—has the greatest name recognition of the five and is the dictionary most often found on reference librarians' desks. However, it is cramped and scrimps on illustrations, with about one-fourth the number in *American Heritage*. Drawing on the huge files of one of the most venerable unabridged dictionaries, *Webster's Third*, it offers somewhat longer definitions than its competitors, but length does not guarantee clarity; the frequent use of illustrative quotations is of more help. *Webster's New Collegiate* does not carry its etymologies particularly far. Priding itself on being descriptive, in particular contrast to *American Heritage*, it dismays the same group that criticizes *Webster's Third*. Collegiate users, however, regret its relative lack of usage level labels. Its prefatory material is definitely a plus.

Webster's Ninth Collegiate Dictionary has just come out and will slowly take the place of *Webster's New Collegiate* on bookstore shelves. (*Webster's New Collegiate* is actually the eighth edition of the basic *Webster's* collegiate dictionary—the title has sometimes included the number of the edition, sometimes not.) Don't assume that bookstores will help you out, the way supermarkets do, by cycling products according to "shelf-

971

pen·tam·e·ter (pĕn-tăm′ə-tər) *n.* **1.** A line of verse composed of five metrical feet. **2.** English verse composed in iambic pentameter; heroic verse. **3.** In Greek and Latin prosody, a line of dactylic verse that constitutes a hexameter with the second halves of the third and sixth feet syncopated and alternates with the hexameters in elegiacs as the latter half of each elegiac couplet. [Old French *pentametre*, from Greek *pentametros* : PENTA- + -METER.]

pen·tane (pĕn′tān′) *n.* Any of three isomeric hydrocarbons, C_5H_{12}, of the methane series: **a.** *Normal pentane.* A colorless flammable liquid used as an anesthetic, a general solvent, and in the manufacture of artificial ice. **b.** *Isopentane.* A colorless flammable liquid used as a solvent and in the manufacture of polystyrene foam. **c.** *Neopentane.* A colorless gas used in the manufacture of synthetic rubber. [PENT(A) + -ANE.]

pen·tan·gu·lar (pĕn-tăng′gyə-lər) *adj.* Having five angles.

pen·ta·quine (pĕn′tə-kwēn′, -kwĭn) *n.* Also **pen·ta·quin** (-kwĭn). A drug used with quinine in the treatment of malaria. [PENTA- + QUIN(OLINE).]

pen·tar·chy (pĕn′tär′kē) *n., pl.* **-chies. 1.** Government by five rulers. **2.** A body of five rulers governing jointly. **3.** An association or federation of five governments, each ruled by a different leader. [Greek *pentarkhia* : PENTA- + -ARCHY.] **—pen·tar′chi·cal** (pĕn-tär′kĭ-kəl) *adj.*

pen·ta·stich (pĕn′tə-stĭk′) *n.* A poem or stanza containing five lines. [Late Greek *pentastikhos*, of five verses : PENTA- + *stikhos,* -STICH.]

Pen·ta·teuch (pĕn′tə-tōōk′, -tyōōk′) *n.* The first five books of the Bible: Genesis, Exodus, Leviticus, Numbers, and Deuteronomy. [Late Latin *Pentateuchus,* from Greek *Pentateukhos* : PENTA- + *teukhos,* a tool, case for papyrus rolls, scroll (see dheugh- in Appendix*).] **—Pen′ta·teuch′al** *adj.*

pen·tath·lon (pĕn-tăth′lən, -lŏn′) *n.* An athletic contest consisting of five events for each participant. Originating in the ancient Olympics, it was revived in the modern Olympics as a series of track and field events. It now consists of running, horseback riding, swimming, fencing, and pistol shooting. [Greek : PENTA- + *athlon,* contest (see **athlete**).]

pen·ta·ton·ic scale (pĕn′tə-tŏn′ĭk). Any of various five-tone musical scales, especially one composed of the first, second, third, fifth, and sixth tones of a diatonic scale.

pen·ta·va·lent (pĕn′tə-vā′lənt) *adj. Chemistry.* Having a valence of 5.

pe·nul·ti·mate (pĭ-nŭl′tə-mĭt) *adj.* **1.** Next to last. **2.** Of or pertaining to the penult of a word: *penultimate stress.* **—n.** The next to the last. [From Latin *paenultimus,* PENULT.]

pe·num·bra (pĭ-nŭm′brə) *n., pl.* **-brae** (-brē) or **-bras. 1.** A partial shadow between regions of complete shadow and complete illumination. The partly darkened fringe around a sunspot. **2.** *Astronomy.* The partly darkened fringe around a sunspot. **3.** An outlying, surrounding region; periphery; fringe: *"Around the core area of Mayan civilization lay a penumbra of other societies"* (William H. McNeill). [New Latin : Latin *paene, pēne,* almost (see **penult**) + UMBRA.] **—pe·num′bral, pe·num′brous** *adj.*

pe·nu·ri·ous (pə-nŏŏr′ē-əs, -nyŏŏr′ē-əs) *adj.* **1.** Miserly; stingy. **2.** Yielding little; barren: *a penurious land.* **3.** Poverty-stricken; needy. [Medieval Latin *pēnūriōsus,* from *pēnūria,* PENURY.] **—pe·nu′ri·ous·ly** *adv.* **—pe·nu′ri·ous·ness** *n.*

pen·u·ry (pĕn′yə-rē) *n.* **1.** Extreme want or poverty; destitution. **2.** Extreme dearth; barrenness; insufficiency. [Middle English, from Latin *paenūria, pēnūria*; want, scarcity.]

Pe·nu·ti·an (pə-nōō′tē-ən, -shən) *n.* A family or phylum of North American Indian languages of Pacific coastal areas from California through British Columbia.

Pen·za (pĕn′zə). A shipping center in the east-central Soviet Union, on the Sura River. Population, 315,000.

Pen·zhi·na (pĕn′zhĭ-nə). A bay of the Sea of Okhotsk extending 185 miles into northeastern Siberia. **2.** A river flowing 446 miles from the Kolyma mountains to this bay.

pe·on (pē′ŏn′, pē′ən; *Spanish* pā-ôn′ *for sense 1; British* pyōōn *for sense 2*) *n., pl.* **peons** or **peones** (pā-ō′nēz; *Spanish* pā-ō′nās). **1. a.** An unskilled laborer or farm worker of Latin America or the southwestern United States. **b.** Such a worker bound in servitude to a landlord creditor. **2.** A native Indian or Ceylonese messenger, servant, or foot soldier. **3.** Any menial worker; a drudge. [Spanish *peon,* Portuguese *pedo* and French *pion,* all from Medieval Latin *pedo* (stem *pedon-*), a foot soldier, from Latin *pēs,* who has broad feet, from *pēs* (stem *ped-*), a foot. See **ped-¹** in Appendix.*]

pe·on·age (pē′ə-nĭj) *n.* Also **pe·on·ism** (-nĭz′əm). **1.** The condition of being a peon. **2.** A system by which debtors are bound in servitude to their creditors until the debts are paid.

pe·o·ny (pē′ə-nē) *n., pl.* **-nies.** Any of various garden plants of the genus *Paeonia,* having large pink, white, or creamy flowers. [Middle English *pione,* Old English *peonie,* from Latin *peōnia,* from Greek *paiōniā,* supposedly discovered by

celebrate the descent of the Holy Ghost upon the disciples. Also called "Whitsunday." **2.** A Jewish festival. **Shavuot** (see). [Middle English *Pentecoste*, Old English *Pentecosten*, from Late Latin *Pentēcostē*, from Greek *pentēkostē (hēmera)*, the fiftieth day (after the Resurrection), Pentecost, from *pentēkostos*, fiftieth, from *pentēkonta*, fifty : *pente*, five (see **penkwe** in Appendix*) + *-konta*, "ten times" (see **dekm** in Appendix*).]

Pen·te·cos·tal (pĕn'tĭ-kôs'tal, -kŏs'tal) *adj.* **1.** Of, pertaining to, or occurring at Pentecost. **2.** Of, pertaining to, or designating any of various Christian religious congregations that seek to be filled with the Holy Ghost, in emulation of the disciples at Pentecost. —**Pen·te·cos·tal** *n.* —**Pen·te·cos·tal·ism** *n.*

pent·house (pĕnt'hous') *n.* **1. a.** An apartment or dwelling situated on the roof of a building. **b.** A residence, often with a terrace, comprising the top floor of an apartment house. **c.** A structure housing machinery on the roof of a building or wall. **2.** A shed or sloping roof attached to the side of a building or wall. [Alteration of Middle English *pentis*, from Old French *appentis*, from Medieval Latin *appenticium*, *appendicium*, appendage, from Latin *appendix*, from *appendere*, to append, attach : *ad-* on + *pendēre*, to suspend, hang (see **spen-** in Appendix*).]

Pent·land Firth (pĕnt'land). A channel between northeastern Scotland and the Orkney Islands.

pent·land·ite (pĕnt'lan-dīt') *n.* The principal ore of nickel. A light-brown nickel iron sulfide. [French: discovered by Joseph B. *Pentland* (died 1873), Irish scientist.]

pen·to·bar·bi·tal sodium (pĕn'tə-bär'bə-tôl'). A white crystalline or powdery barbiturate, $C_{11}H_{17}N_2O_3Na$, used as a sedative. [From PENT(A)- + BARBITAL.]

pen·to·san (pĕn'tə-săn') *n.* Any of a group of complex carbohydrates found in many woody plants and yielding pentoses on hydrolysis. [PENTOS(E) + -AN.]

pen·tose (pĕn'tōs', -tōz') *n.* A sugar having five carbon atoms per molecule. [PENT(A)- + -OSE.]

Pen·to·thal Sodium (pĕn'tə-thôl'). A trademark for a drug, thiopental sodium (see).

pent·ox·ide (pĕnt-ŏk'sīd') *n.* An oxide having five atoms of oxygen in the molecule. [PENT(A)- + OXIDE.]

pent·ste·mon. Variant of penstemon.

pent·up (pĕnt'ŭp') *adj.* Not given expression; repressed: *pent-up emotions.*

pen·tyl (pĕn'tal) *n. Chemistry.* Amyl (see). [PENT(A)- + -YL.]

pen·tyl·ene·tet·ra·zol (pĕn'tə-lēn'tĕt'rə-zōl', -zŏl') *n.* A drug, $C_6H_{10}N_4$, used as a stimulant of the central nervous system. [PENT(A)- + (METH)YLENE + TETR(A)- + AZ(O)- + -OL.]

pe·nu·che (pə-nōo'chē) *n.* Also **pe·nu·chi.** A fudgelike confection of brown sugar, water or milk, and chopped nuts. Also called "panocha." [Mexican Spanish *panocha*, diminutive of Spanish *pan*, bread, from Latin *pānis.* See **pā-** in Appendix*.]

pe·nuch·le, pe·nuck·le. Variants of pinochle.

pe·nult (pē'nŭlt', pĭ-nŭlt') *n.* Also **pe·nul·ti·ma** (pĭ-nŭl'tə-ma). The next to the last syllable in a word. [Latin *paenultimus*, last but one : *paene*, *pēner*, almost + *ultimus*, farthest away, last, from *uls*, beyond (see **al-¹** in Appendix*).]

body of persons living in the same country under one national government; nationality. **2.** A body of persons sharing a common religion, culture, language, or inherited condition of life. **3.** Persons with regard to their residence, class, profession, or group. **4.** The mass of ordinary persons; the populace. Usually preceded by *the*: "*and what the people but a herd confus'd,/ a miscellaneous rabble*" (Milton). **5.** The citizens of a nation, state, or other political unit; electorate. See Usage note below. **6.** Persons subordinate to or loyal to a ruler, superior, or employer. **7.** Family, relatives, or ancestors. **8.** Members of the community; persons in general. **9.** Human beings considered as distinct from lower animals or inanimate things. **10.** A race or kind of beings distinct from human beings: *the little people.* —See Synonyms at **nation.** —*tr.v.* **peopled, -pling, -ples.** To furnish, with a population; populate. [Middle English *peple, peeple*, from Old French *pueple, pueple*, from Latin *populus*. See **populus** in Appendix*.] —**peo'pler** *n.*

Usage: The possessive form is usually *people's* (*the people's rights*), but *peoples'* is the possessive of the plural form *peoples* (*the Semitic peoples' interests*). *People* (not *persons*) is the proper term when referring to a large group of individuals collectively and indefinitely: *People can be pushed only so far. Persons* is applicable to a specific and relatively small number: *Ten persons were killed.* But *people* is also acceptable in this example. *The people* and *the public* are sometimes interchangeable, but only *the people* has the political sense of an electorate.

people's front. A political coalition, popular front (see).

People's Party. The Populist Party (see).

People's Republic of China. The official name for China (see).

Pe·o·ri·a (pē-ôr'ē-ə, -ōr'ē-ə). A city in north-central Illinois, on the Illinois River, 67 miles north of Springfield. Population, 127,000.

pep (pĕp) *n. Informal.* Energy; high spirits; vim. —*tr.v.* **pepped, pepping. peps.** *Informal.* To bring energy or liveliness to; invigorate. Usually followed by *up.* [Short for PEPPER.] —**pep'py** *adj.* —**pep'pi·ness** *n.*

Pep·in the Short (pĕp'ĭn). A.D. 714?-768. King of the Franks (751-768); son of Charles Martel and father of Charlemagne.

pep·los (pĕp'lăs, -lŏs') *n., pl.* **-loses.** Also **pep·lus** (pĕp'ləs). A loose outer robe worn by women in ancient Greece. Also called "peplum." [Greek *peplos.*]

pep·lum (pĕp'ləm) *n., pl.* **-lums. 1.** A short overskirt or ruffle attached at the waistline. **2.** A peplos (see). [Latin, from *peplus, peplos*, from Greek *peplos*, PEPLOS.]

pe·po (pē'pō) *n., pl.* **-pos.** The fruit of any of various related plants, such as the cucumber, squash, pumpkin, and melon, having a hard rind, fleshy pulp, and numerous seeds. [Latin, melon, from Greek *pepōn.* See **pekw-** in Appendix.*]

pep·per (pĕp'ər) *n.* **1.** A woody vine, *Piper nigrum*, of the East Indies, having small, berrylike fruit. **2.** The dried, blackish fruit of this plant, used as a pungent condiment. When ground whole, it is called *black pepper*, and with the shell removed, *white pepper.* **3.** Any of several other plants of the genus *Piper*, such as cubeb, betel, and kava. **4.** Any of several varieties of a

of the Amazons who aided the Trojans against the Greeks and was killed by Achilles.

pent·house (pent'hous') *n.* **1.** An apartment or dwelling on the roof of a building. **2.** A structure built on a roof to conceal or cover a water tank, elevator machinery, etc. **3.** A small building, or a sloping rooflike structure, attached to the wall of another building. **4.** A canopy or awning above a doorway or window. [Alter. of ME *pentis*, aphetic form of OF *apentis, apendis,* ? < LL *appendicium* appendage < L *appendere.* See APPEND.]

pen·tom·ic (pen·tom'ik) *adj. Mil.* Of or designating a U.S. Army division designed primarily for use in nuclear warfare and consisting of five self-contained battle groups of high mobility, supported by atomic weapons. [< PENT(A) + (AT)OMIC]

pen·to·san (pen'tə·san) *n. Biochem.* One of a group of polysaccharides, found in foods and plant juices, that yield pentoses on hydrolysis. [< PENTOS(E) + -AN]

pen·tose (pen'tōs) *n. Biochem.* Any of a class of monosaccharides having five carbon atoms in the molecule. [< Gk. *pent(e)* five + -OSE²]

Pen·to·thal Sodium (pen'tə·thôl) A proprietary name for a brand of thiopental sodium. Also **pen'to·thal sodium.**

pent·ste·mon (pent·stē'mən, pent'stem·ən) See PENSTEMON.

pent-up (pent'up') *adj.* Confined; repressed: *pent-up emotions.*

pe·nu·che (pə·nōō'chē) *n.* A candy made from brown sugar and milk, often with chopped nuts: also called *panocha.* Also **pe·nu'chi.** [< Am. Sp. *panocha* brown or raw sugar]

pe·nuch·le (pē'nuk·əl), **pe·nuck·le** See PINOCHLE.

pe·nult (pē'nult, pi·nult') *n.* The syllable next to the last in a word. Also **pe·nul·ti·ma** (pi·nul'tə·mə). [Short for *penultima* < L *paenultima (syllaba)* next to the last (syllable) < *paene* almost + *ultimus* last]

pe·nul·ti·mate (pi·nul'tə·mit) *adj.* **1.** Next to the last. **2.** Of or belonging to the next to the last syllable. — *n.* A penultimate syllable or part. [< L *paene* almost + ULTIMATE, on analogy with L *paenultimus* next to the last]

pe·num·bra (pi·num'brə) *n., pl.* **·brae** (-brē) or **·bras** **1.** A partial shadow within which the rays of light from an illuminating body are partly but not wholly intercepted. **2.** *Astron.* **a** In an eclipse, the partial shadow between the region of total eclipse and the region of unobstructed light. **b** The dark fringe around the central part of a sunspot. **3.** In painting, the point or line at which light and shade are

relatives. **9.** Human beings as distinguished from animals. **10.** Animals collectively: *the ant people.* — **good people.** In Ireland, the fairies: also **little people.** — *v.t.* **·pled, ·pling** To fill with inhabitants; populate. [< OF *purple, poeple* < L *populus* populace] — **peo'pler** *n.*

— **Syn.** *People, folk, nation, population,* and *race* are compared as they denote a large number of persons collectively. A group having a common descent, language, culture, habitat, or government may be called a *people;* this word evades stress on any one aspect, but may also be used in a more restricted sense to indicate specifically an ethnic, cultural, linguistic, or other community. *Folk* is a homelier word for *people,* nearly as broad, and usually stressing common traditions, customs, or behavior. A *nation* is a political entity, comprising the *people* (or *peoples*) under one government. *Population* refers to habitat, and comprises all the members of a group found in one region; it is the only one of the synonyms commonly used of human and nonhuman groups alike. *Race* refers to descent, and includes all those of roughly similar physical features who are considered to have a common ancestry. Compare TRIBE.

People's front A popular front (which see).

People's Party A political organization formed in the United States in 1891, and advocating an increase in currency, free coinage of silver, public control of railways, an income tax, and limitation of ownership of land: also called *Populist Party.*

Pe·o·ri·a (pē·ôr'ē·ə, -ō'rē·ə) A city in north central Illinois, on the Illinois River; pop. 126,963.

pep (pep) *n. Informal* Energy and high spirits; vigorous activity. — *v.t.* **pepped, pep·ping** To fill or inspire with energy or pep: usually with *up.* [Short for PEPPER]

Pep·in the Short (pep'in). died 768, king of the Franks 751–768; father of Charlemagne.

pep·los (pep'los) *n.* In ancient Greece, a woman's shawl or large scarf worn draped about the upper part of the body: also *peplum.* Also **pep'lus.** [< Gk.]

pep·lum (pep'lam) *n., pl.* **·lums** or **·la** (-lə) **1.** A short overskirt, ruffle, or flounce attached to a blouse or coat at the waist, and extending down over the hips. **2.** A peplos. [< L < Gk. *peplos* peplos]

pe·po (pē'pō) *n., pl.* **·pos** The fleshy fruit of plants of the gourd family, with hardened rind and numerous enclosed seeds, as the squash, cucumber, pumpkin, melon, etc. Also **pe·pon·i·da** (pi·pon'ə·də), **pe·po·mi·um** (pi·pō'nē·əm). [< L pumpkin < Gk. *pepōn (sikyos)* ripe (gourd)]

pep·per (pep'ər) *n.* **1.** A pungent, aromatic condiment consisting of the dried immature berries of a plant (*Piper*

needy; **3.** Affording or yielding little; scanty. [< MF *penurieux* < Med.L *penuriosus* < L *penuria* want, poverty] — **pe·nu·ri·ous·ly** *adv.* — **pe·nu·ri·ous·ness** *n.*

pen·u·ry (pen′yə-rē) *n.* Extreme poverty or want. [< OF *penurie* < L *penuria* want]
— **Syn.** indigence, destitution, need.

Pe·nu·ti·an (pə-nōō′tē-ən, -shən) *n.* A phylum of northwestern North American Indian languages, including the Chinookan and Shahaptian linguistic stocks.

Pen·za (pyen′za) A city in the western R.S.F.S.R., on the Sura: pop. 254,000 (1959).

Pen·zance (pen-zans′) A municipal borough and port in western Cornwall, England; pop. 19,433 (1961).

pe·on (pē′ən) *n.* **1.** In Latin America: **a** A laborer; servant. **b** Formerly, a debtor kept in servitude until he had worked out of his debt. **2.** In India: **a** A foot soldier. **b** A messenger, attendant, or orderly. **c** A native police officer or constable.
— **Syn.** See SLAVE. [< Sp. *peón* < LL *pedo, -onis* foot soldier < L *pes, pedis* foot. Doublet of PAWN[1].]

pe·on·age (pē′ən-ij) *n.* **1.** The condition of being a peon. **2.** The system by which debtors are held in servitude until they have worked out their debt. Also **pe′on·ism** (-iz′əm).

pe·o·ny (pē′ə-nē) *n. pl.* **·nies 1.** Any of a genus (*Paeonia*) of plants of the crowfoot family, having large crimson, rose, or white flowers. **2.** The flower. [OE *peonie* < L *paeonia* < Gk. *paiōnia* < *Paion* Paeon, the Healer]

peo·ple (pē′pəl) *n. pl.* **peo·ple;** *for defs. 1 & 2, also* **peo·ples 1.** The entire body of human beings living in the same country, under the same government, and speaking the same language: the *people* of England. **2.** A body of human beings having the same history, culture, and traditions, and usually speaking the same language: the Polish *people.* **3.** In a state or nation, the whole body of persons invested with political rights; the enfranchised. **4.** A group or body of persons having the same interests, profession, condition of life, place of residence, etc.: poor *people.* **5.** Persons considered collectively and not as individuals: *people* say. **6.** Ordinary persons as distinguished from those who are wealthy, privileged, titled, etc.; the populace: usually with *the.* **7.** Those persons connected with someone as subjects, attendants, etc.: the Queen's *people.* **8.** One's family or

pepper (which see). **4.** Green pepper (which see). — *v.t.* **1.** To sprinkle or season with pepper. **2.** To sprinkle freely. **3.** To shower, as with missiles; spatter; pelt. **4.** To make (speech or writing) vivid or pungent, as with humor, sarcasm, etc. — *v.i.* **5.** To discharge missiles at something [OE *pipor*, ult. < L *piper* < Gk. *peperi.* Cf. Skt. *pippali* peppercorn.]

pep·per-and-salt (pep′ər-ən-sôlt′) *adj.* Having or consisting of a mixture of white and black, so intermingled as to present a grayish appearance: said of cloth, hair, etc. — *n.* A pepper-and-salt cloth.

pep·per·box (pep′ər-boks′) *n.* **1.** A cylindrical container with a perforated lid for sprinkling pepper. **2.** A quick-tempered person.

pep·per·corn (pep′ər-kôrn′) *n.* **1.** A berry of the pepper plant. **2.** Anything trifling or insignificant.

pep·per·grass (pep′ər-gras′, -gräs′) *n.* Any of a genus (*Lepidium*) of plants of the mustard family, having a pungent flavor, and used as a salad vegetable. Also **pep′per·wort** (-wûrt).

pep·per·idge (pep′ər-ij) *n.* The black gum, a tree. [Origin unknown]

pepper mill A hand mill, often designed for table use, in which peppercorns are ground.

pep·per·mint (pep′ər-mint′) *n.* **1.** A pungent, aromatic herb (*Mentha piperita*), used in medicine and confectionery. **2.** An oil or other preparation made from this herb. **3.** A confection flavored with peppermint.

pepper pot 1. A pepperbox. **2.** A West Indian stew of meat or fish with okra, chilis, and other vegetables, flavored with Cayenne pepper, etc. **3.** In the United States, a soup of tripe and vegetables, highly seasoned with pepper.

pep·per·root (pep′ər-rōōt′, -rŏŏt′) *n.* Crinkleroot (which see).

pepper tree 1. A Tasmanian and Australian shrub (*Drimys aromatica*) of the magnolia family, having small, greenish yellow flowers and globular berries sometimes used as a substitute for pepper. **2.** A tree (*Schinus molle*), of Central and South America, whose seeds are used as a spice and whose fruit yields an intoxicating beverage: also called *Peruvian mastic.*

PRONUNCIATION KEY: add, āce, câre, pälm; end, ēven; it, īce; odd, ōpen, ôrder; tŏŏk, pōōl; up, bûrn; ə = a in *above*, e in *sicken*, i in *flexible*, o in *melon*, u in *focus*; yōō = u in *fuse*; oil; pout; check; go; ring; thin; this; zh, vision. For à, œ, ü, kh, ñ, see inside front cover.

which are cultivated for their showy flowers. Also, **penste-mon.** [< NL = *pent-* PENT- + Gk *stēmōn* warp, thread]
pent-up (pĕnt'ŭp'), *adj.* confined; restrained; curbed: *pent-up emotions.*
pen'tyl group', *Chem.* any of the univalent, isomeric groups having the formula C₅H₁₁–.
pe-nu-che (pə nōō'chē), *n.* 1. Also, **panocha,** a candy made of brown sugar, butter, and milk, usually with nuts. 2. panocha (def. 1). [var. of PANOCHA]
pe-nult (pē'nult, pĭ nult'), *n.* the next to the last syllable in a word. Also, **pe-nul-ti-ma** (pĭ nul'tə mə). [< L *paenul-(tima)* (*syllaba*), contr. of *paene ultima* almost the last; see ULTIMA]
pe-nul-ti-mate (pĭ nul'tə mĭt), *adj.* 1. next to the last. 2. of or pertaining to a penult or penults. —*n.* 3. a penult.
pe-num-bra (pĭ num'brə), *n.,* *pl.* **-brae** (-brē), **-bras.** 1. the partial or imperfect shadow surrounding the complete shadow of an opaque body. Cf. umbra (def. 3). 2. the grayish marginal portion of a sunspot. Cf. umbra (def. 4). [< NL]
—**pe-num'bral, pe-num'brous,** *adj.*
pe-nu-ri-ous (pə nŏŏr'ē əs, -nyŏŏr'-), *adj.* 1. extremely stingy. 2. extremely poor; indigent. 3. poorly or inadequately supplied. [< ML *penūri(us)*. See PENURY, -OUS]
—**pe-nu'ri-ous-ly,** *adv.* —**pe-nu'ri-ous-ness,** *n.* —Syn. 1. tight, close, niggardly. —Ant. 1. generous.
pen-u-ry (pen'yə rē), *n.* 1. extreme poverty. 2. scarcity; insufficiency. [late ME < L *pēnūria,* akin to Gk *peīna* hunger, *penía* poverty] —Syn. 1. indigence, need, want.
Pe-nu-ti-an (pə nōō'tē ən, -shən), *n.* 1. a North American Indian linguistic stock, tentatively established as being distributed from California northward through Oregon and British Columbia. —*adj.* 2. of or pertaining to Penutian. [*Penuti* (learned coinage, combining *pen* two and *uti* two, taken from different languages of the stock) + -AN]
Pen-za (pen'zä), *n.* a city in the W RSFSR, in the central Soviet Union in Europe. 305,000 (1964).
Pen-zance (pen zans'), *n.* a seaport in SW Cornwall, in the SW extremity of England; resort. 19,433 (1961).
pe-on¹ (pē'ən, pē'on), *n.* 1. (in Spanish America and southwestern U.S.) a. a person who tends a horse or mule. b. See day laborer. 2. (esp. in Mexico) a person held in servitude to work off debts or other obligations. [< Sp *peón* peasant, day laborer < VL **pedōn-* (s. of **pedō*) walker (> ML *pedōnes* infantry, OF *peon* pawn) < L *ped-* (s. of *pēs*) foot]
pe-on² (pē'ən, pē'on), *n.* (in India and Ceylon) 1. a messenger or attendant. 2. a native soldier. 3. See foot soldier. See PEON¹.
[< Pg *peão,* F *pion* foot soldier, pedestrian, day laborer. See PEON¹]
pe-on-age (pē'ə nĭj), *n.* 1. the condition or service of a peon. 2. the practice of holding persons in servitude or partial slavery, as to work off a debt or to serve a penal sentence.
pe-on-ism (pē'ə nĭz'əm), *n. Archaic.* peonage.
pe-o-ny (pē'ə nē), *n.,* *pl.* **-nies.** 1. any ranunculaceous herb or shrub of the genus *Paeonia,* having large, showy flowers. 2. the flower; the state flower of Indiana. [ME *pione* < AF, OE *peonie* < LL *peōnia,* L *paeōnia* < Gk *paiōnía* peony, akin to *paiōnios* healing]

fine mixture of black with white, as cloth.
pep-per-box (pep'ər boks'), *n.* a small box with perforations in the top, for sprinkling pepper. Also called **pepper pot.**
pep-per-corn (pep'ər kôrn'), *n.* 1. the berry of the pepper plant, *Piper nigrum,* dried and used as a spice, often after being ground. 2. anything very small, insignificant, or trifling. —*adj.* 3. (of hair) growing in tightly spiraled clumps. [ME *pepercorn* < OE *piporcorn*] —**pep'per-corn'ish, pep'per-corn'y,** *adj.*
pep-per-grass (pep'ər gras', -gräs'), *n.* any pungent plant of the genus *Lepidium,* used as a potherb or salad vegetable. Cf. **garden cress.**
pep-per-idge (pep'ər ĭj), *n.* the tupelo. [?]
pep-per-mill (pep'ər mĭl'), *n.* a small hand mill for grinding peppercorns in the kitchen or at the table.
pep-per-mint (pep'ər mint'), *n.* 1. a labiate herb, *Mentha piperita,* cultivated for its aromatic, pungent oil. 2. Also called **pep'permint oil',** this oil, or some preparation of it. 3. a lozenge or confection flavored with it.
pep-per-o-ni (pep'ə rō'nē), *n.* peperoni.
pep'per pot', 1. a West Indian stew, the principal flavoring of which is cassareep, with meat or fish and vegetables. 2. a highly seasoned soup made of tripe and vegetables. 3. pepperbox.
pep'per tree', any of several chiefly South American, evergreen trees of the genus *Schinus,* cultivated in subtropical regions as an ornamental.
pep-per-y (pep'ə rē), *adj.* 1. full of or tasting like pepper. 2. of, pertaining to, or resembling pepper. 3. sharp or stinging; peppery speech. 4. easily angered; irritable; irascible. —**pep'per-i-ly,** *adv.* —**pep'per-i-ness,** *n.* —Syn. 1. spicy. 3. biting. —**pep'per,** hot-tempered, testy. —Ant. 1. mild, bland.
pep'pill', a pill, tablet, or capsule that consists typically of a form of the stimulant drug amphetamine.
pep-py (pep'ē), *adj.,* **-pi-er, -pi-est.** *Informal.* energetic; vigorous; lively. —**pep'pi-ly,** *adv.* —**pep'pi-ness,** *n.*
pep-sin (pep'sin), *n. Biochem.* 1. an enzyme, produced in the stomach, that in the presence of hydrochloric acid splits proteins into proteoses and peptones. 2. a commercial form of this substance, used as a digestive, as a ferment in the manufacture of cheese, etc. Also, **pep'sine.** [< Gk *pépsi(s)* digestion (*péptein*) (to) digest + *-sis* -sis) + -IN²]
pep-sin-ate (pep'sə nāt'), *v.t.,* **-at-ed, -at-ing.** to treat, prepare, or mix with pepsin.
pep-sin-o-gen (pep sin'ə jən), *n. Biochem.* a zymogen, occurring in the gastric glands, that during digestion is converted into pepsin. —**pep-si-no-gen-ic** (pep'sə nō jen'ĭk), *adj.*
pep-si-nog-e-nous (pep'sə noj'ə nəs), *adj.*
pep' talk', a vigorous talk, as to a person or group, calculated to arouse support for a cause, increase the determination to succeed, etc.
pep-tic (pep'tĭk), *adj.* 1. pertaining to or associated with digestion; digestive. 2. promoting digestion. 3. of or pertaining to pepsin. —*n.* 4. a substance promoting digestion. [< Gk *peptik(ós)* conducive to digestion = *pept(ós)* digested (verbid of *péptein*) + *-ikos* -IC]
pep'tic ul'cer, an erosion of the mucous membrane of

etc. **4.** a person's family or relatives. **5.** the fellow members of one's group or community. **6.** the body of enfranchised citizens of a state. **7.** the ordinary persons of a community, as distinguished from rulers, officials, etc. **8.** persons indefinitely: *Won't people gossip?* **9.** human beings, as distinguished from animals. —*v.t.* **10.** to furnish with people; populate. **11.** to settle in or inhabit. [ME *peple* < AF *people*, OF *pueple* < L *populus*). See POPULAR] —**Syn. 1.** See **race²**.

peo'ple mov'er, any of various experimental mass-transit systems whose general concept is the use of horizontal moving belts or unconventional vehicles to transport people around airports, shopping areas, etc.

Peo'ple's com'mune, a usually rural, Communist Chinese social and administrative unit of from 2000 to 4000 families combined for collective farming, fishing, mining, or industrial projects. Also called **commune.**

Peo'ple's Par'ty, *U.S. Politics.* a political party (1891–1904), advocating expansion of currency, state control of railroads, etc.

Pe·o·ri·a (pē ôr′ē ə, -ōr′-), *n.* a city in central Illinois, on the Illinois River. 126,963 (1970). —**Pe·o′ri·an,** *adj., n.*

pep (pep), *n., v.,* **pepped, pep·ping.** *Informal.* —*n.* **1.** spirit or animation; vigor; energy. —*v.t.* **2. pep up,** to make or become vigorous or lively. [short for PEPPER]

pep·er·o·ni (pep′ə rō′nē), *n.* a highly seasoned, hard sausage of beef and pork. Also, **pepperoni.** Also, *pepe* PEPPER]

Pep·in (pep′in), *n.* (*"Pepin the Short"*) died A.D. 768, king of the Franks 751–768 (father of Charlemagne).

pep·los (pep′ləs), *n., pl.* **-los·es.** a voluminous outer garment worn, draped in folds, by women in ancient Greece. Also, **peplus.** [< Gk]

pep·lum (pep′ləm), *n., pl.* **-lums, -la** (-lə). **1.** a short full flounce or an extension of a garment below the waist, covering the hips. **2.** a short skirt attached to a bodice or jacket. [< L < Gk **peplon* (only pl. *pēpla* occurs). See PEPLOS]

pep·lus (pep′ləs), *n., pl.* **-lus·es.** peplos.

pep·o (pē′pō), *n., pl.* **-pos.** the characteristic fruit of cucurbitaceous plants, having a fleshy, many-seeded interior and a hard or firm rind, as the gourd, melon, cucumber, etc. [< L: large melon, pumpkin < Gk *pépōn,* short for *pépōn* (síkyos) a ripe (gourd)]

pep·per (pep′ər), *n.* **1.** a pungent condiment obtained from various plants of the genus *Piper,* esp. from the dried berries of the tropical, climbing shrub *P. nigrum.* **2.** any plant of the genus *Piper,* or the family *Piperaceae.* **3.** cayenne, or red pepper, prepared from species of Capsicum. **4.** any plant of the genus *Capsicum,* esp. the common garden pepper, *C. frutescens,* or its green or red, hot or sweet fruit. —*v.t.* **5.** to season with or as with pepper. **6.** to sprinkle with or as with pepper; dot; stud. **7.** to pelt with shot or missiles. [ME *pepper,* OE *pipar* < L < Gk *péperi;* cf. D *peper,* G *Pfeffer,* Icel *piparr*]

pep·per-and-salt (pep′ər ən sôlt′), *adj.* composed of a

to amino acids.

pep·tide (pep′tīd, -tid), *n.* *Biochem.* a compound containing two or more amino acids in which the carboxyl group of one acid is linked to the amino group of the other, as H₂NCH₂CONHCH₂COOH. [PEPT(IC) + -IDE]

pep·tize (pep′tīz), *v.t.,* **-tized, -tiz·ing.** to disperse (a substance) into colloidal form, usually in a liquid. [? < Gk *pēpt(ein)* (to) digest + -IZE] —**pep·tiz′a·ble,** *adj.* —**pep′-tiz·a′tion,** *n.* —**pep′tiz·er,** *n.*

pep·tone (pep′tōn), *n.* *Biochem.* any of a class of diffusible, soluble substances into which proteins are converted by partial hydrolysis. [< G *Pepton* < Gk *peptón,* neut. of *peptós* cooked, digested, verbal of *péptein*] —**pep·ton·ic** (pep-tŏn′ĭk), *adj.* —**pep′to·noid** (pep′tə noid′), *n.*

pep·to·nize (pep′tə nīz′), *v.t.,* **-nized, -niz·ing.** *Chiefly Brit.* peptonize. —**pep′to·ni·za′tion,** *n.* —**pep′to·niz′er,** *n.*

pep·to·nize (pep′tə nīz′), *v.t.,* **-nized, -niz·ing.** to hydrolyze or dissolve by a proteolytic enzyme, as pepsin. —**pep′-to·ni·za′tion,** *n.*

Pep·ys (pēps, peps, pep′is, pep′ēs), *n.* **Samuel,** 1633–1703, English diarist and naval official.

Pe·quot (pē′kwot), *n., pl.* **-quots,** (esp. collectively) **-quot.** a member of a former tribe of Algonquin Indians, in southern New England in the early 17th century. [? shortened var. of Narragansett *paquatanog* destroyers]

per (pûr; unstressed pər), *prep.* for each; through; by: *12 parts per thousand.* [< L, ML, OF: through, by, for, for each. See [PRO²]

—**Usage.** In commercial use **a** is preferred to PER by most stylists: *$40 a gross; 5 percent interest a year.*

per-, **1.** a prefix meaning "through," "thoroughly," "utterly," "very": *pervert; pervade; perfect.* **2.** *Chem.* a prefix applied to inorganic acids and their salts to indicate that they possess an excess of the designated element: *percarbonic acid* (H₂C₂O₅); *permanganic acid* (HMnO₄); *potassium permanganate* (KMnO₄); *potassium persulfate* (K₂S₂O₈). [< L, comb. form of *per* PER, and used as an intensive]

Per., **1.** Persia. **2.** Persian.

per., **1.** period. **2.** person.

Pe·ra (pe′rä), *n.* a modern section of Istanbul, Turkey, N of the Golden Horn. 218,433 (1965). Also called **Beyoglu.**

per·ac·id (pər as′id), *n.* *Chem.* an oxyacid, the primary element of which is in its highest possible oxidation state, as perchloric acid, HClO₄, and permanganic acid, HMnO₄.

per·ad·ven·ture (pûr′əd ven′chər, per′-), *n.* **1.** chance or uncertainty. **2.** surmise. —*adv.* **3.** *Archaic.* it may be; maybe; possibly; perhaps. [ME *per aventure* < OF]

Pe·rae·a (pə rē′ə), *n.* a region in ancient Palestine. E of the Jordan and the Dead Sea.

Pe·rak (pā′räk, -rĭk, pɛr′ə, pēr′ə), *n.* a state in Malaysia, on the SW Malay Peninsula. 1,384,321 (est. 1961); 7080 sq. mi. *Cap.* Taiping.

per·am·bu·late (pər am′byə lāt′), *v.,* **-lat·ed, -lat·ing.** —*v.t.* **1.** to walk through, about, or over; travel through;

pepper 1b

pen·to·bar·bi·tal \pent-ə-ˈbär-bə-ˌtȯl\ n [penta- + -ō- + barbital] : a granular barbiturate $C_{11}H_{18}N_2O_3$ used esp. in the form of its sodium or calcium salt as a sedative, hypnotic, and antispasmodic
pen·to·bar·bi·tone \-ˌtōn\ n [penta- + -ō- + barbitone (barbital)] Brit : PENTOBARBITAL

pen·tom·ic \pen-ˈtäm-ik\ adj [blend of penta- and atomic] 1 : made up of five battle groups (a ~ division) 2 : organized into pentomic divisions (a ~ army)

pen·to·san \ˈpent-ə-ˌsan\ n : any of various polysaccharides that yield only pentoses on hydrolysis and are widely distributed in plants

pen·tose \ˈpen-ˌtōs, -ˌtōz\ n [ISV] : any of various monosaccharides $C_5H_{10}O_5$ (as ribose) that contain five carbon atoms in the molecule
pen·to·side \ˈpent-ə-ˌsīd\ n : a glycoside that yields a pentose on hydrolysis

Pen·to·thal \ˈpent-ə-ˌthȯl\ trademark — used for thiopental
pent·ox·ide \pent-ˈäk-ˌsīd\ n [ISV] : an oxide containing five atoms of oxygen in the molecule

pent·ste·mon or **pen·ste·mon** \pent-ˈstē-mən, ˈpen(t)-stə-\ n [NL pentstemon, alter. of Penstemon, genus name, fr. Gk penta- + stēmōn thread — more at STAMEN] : any of a genus (Penstemon) of chiefly American herbs of the figwort family with showy blue, purple, red, yellow, or white flowers

pen·tyl \ˈpent-ᵊl\ n [pentane + -yl] : AMYL
pen·tyl·ene·tet·ra·zol \ˌpent-ᵊl-ˌēn-ˈte-trə-ˌzȯl, -ˌzōl\ n [pentyl + amethylene-tetrazole] : a compound $C_6H_{10}N_4$ used as a respiratory and circulatory stimulant and for producing a state of convulsion in treating mental disorders

pe·nu·che \pə-ˈnü-chē\ n [MexSp panocha raw sugar, fr. dim. of Sp pan bread, fr. L panis — more at FOOD] : fudge made usu. of brown sugar, butter, cream or milk, and nuts

pe·nult \ˈpē-nəlt, pi-ˈ\ n [L paenultima penult, fr. fem. of paenultimus almost last, fr. paene almost + ultimus last] : the next to the last member of a series; esp : the next to the last syllable of a word
pen·ul·ti·ma \pi-ˈnəl-tə-mə\ n [L] : PENULT
pen·ul·ti·mate \pi-ˈnəl-tə-mət\ adj 1 : next to the last (the ~ chapter of a book) 2 : of or relating to a penult (a ~ accent) — **pen·ul·ti·mate·ly** adv

pen·um·bra \pə-ˈnəm-brə\ n, pl -brae \-ˌ)brē, -ˌbrī\ or -bras [NL, fr. L paene almost + umbra shadow — more at PATIENT, UMBRAGE] 1 : a space of partial illumination (as in an eclipse) between the perfect shadow on all sides and the full light 2 : a shaded region surrounding the dark central portion of a sunspot 3 : a surrounding or adjoining region in which something exists in a lesser degree : FRINGE — **pen·um·bral** \-brəl\ adj

pe·nu·ri·ous \pə-ˈn(y)u̇r-ē-əs\ adj 1 : marked by or suffering from penury 2 : given to or marked by extreme stinting frugality syn see STINGY — **pe·nu·ri·ous·ly** adv — **pe·nu·ri·ous·ness** n
pen·u·ry \ˈpen-yə-rē\ n [ME, fr. L penuria want — more at PATIENT] 1 : a cramping and oppressive lack of resources (as money); esp

carminative, or stimulant: (1) : BLACK PEPPER (2) : WHITE PEPPER **b** : any of a genus (Piper of the family Piperaceae, the pepper family) of tropical mostly jointed climbing shrubs with aromatic leaves; esp : a woody vine (P. nigrum) with ovate leaves and spicate flowers that is widely cultivated in the tropics for its red berries from which black pepper and white pepper are prepared 2 **a** : any of several products similar to pepper that are obtained from close relatives of the pepper plant **b** : any of various pungent condiments obtained from plants of other genera than that of the pepper — used with a qualifying term (cayenne ~) 3 **a** : CAPSICUM 1; esp : a New World capsicum (Capsicum frutescens) whose fruits are hot peppers or sweet peppers **b** : the usu. red or yellow fruit of a pepper — **pepper** adj

²**pepper** vt **pep·pered**; **pep·per·ing** \ˈpep-(ə-)riŋ\ 1 **a** : to sprinkle, season, or cover with or as if with pepper **b** : to shower with shot or other missiles 2 : to hit with rapid repeated blows 3 : to sprinkle as pepper is sprinkled (~ed his report with statistics) — **pep·per·er** \-ər-ər\ n

pep·per-and-salt \ˌpep-ər-(ə)n-ˈsȯlt\ adj : having black and white or dark and light color intermingled in small flecks (a ~ overcoat)
pep·per·box \ˈpep-ər-ˌbäks\ n 1 : a small usu. cylindrical box or bottle with a perforated top used for sprinkling ground pepper on food 2 : a small cylindrical tower or turret 3 : a late 18th century pistol with five or six revolving barrels

pep·per·corn \-ˌkȯ(ə)rn\ n : a dried berry of the black pepper
pep·pered moth n : a European geometrid moth (Biston betularia) that typically has white wings with small black specks but also occurs as a solid black form late in areas where the air is heavily polluted by industry

pep·per·grass \ˈpep-ər-ˌgras\ n : any of a genus (Lepidium) of cresses; esp : GARDEN CRESS

pepper mill n : a hand mill for grinding peppercorns
pep·per·mint \-ˌmint, -mənt\ n, often cap **a** : a pungent and aromatic mint (Mentha piperita) with dark green lanceolate leaves and whorls of small pink flowers in spikes **b** : any of several mints (as M. arvensis) that are related to the peppermint 2 : candy flavored with peppermint — **pep·per·min·ty** \ˈpep-ər-ˌmint-ē\ adj

pep·per·o·ni \ˌpep-ə-ˈrō-nē\ n, [It peperoni chilies, pl. of peperone chili, aug. of pepe pepper, fr. L piper — more at PEPPER] : a highly seasoned beef and pork sausage

pepper pot n 1 Brit : PEPPERBOX 2 **a** : a highly seasoned West Indian stew of vegetables and meat or fish **b** : a thick soup of

ons or **pe·o·nes** \pä-'ō-nēz\ n [Pg peao & F pion, fr. ML pedon-, pedo foot soldier — more at PAWN] **1**: any of various Indian or Ceylonese workers: as **a**: INFANTRYMAN **b**: ORDERLY **2** [Sp peón, fr. L pedon-, pedo]: a member of the landless laboring class in Spanish America **3** pl peons **a**: a person held in compulsory servitude for the working out of an indebtedness **b**: DRUDGE, MENIAL

pe·on·age \'pē-ə-nij\ n **1**: the condition of a peon **2 a**: the use of laborers bound in servitude because of debt **b**: a system of convict labor by which convicts are leased to contractors

pe·o·ny \'pē-ə-nē\ n, pl -nies [ME piony, fr. L paeonia, fr. Gk paiōnia, fr. Paiōn Paeon, physician of the gods]: any of a genus (Paeonia) of plants of the buttercup family with large usu. double flowers of red, pink, or white

peo·ple \'pē-pal\ n, pl people [ME peple, fr. OF peuple, fr. L populus] **1** pl: HUMAN BEINGS, PERSONS — often used in compounds instead of persons ⟨salespeople⟩ **2** pl: human beings making up a group or assembly or linked by a common interest **3** pl: the members of a family or kinship **4** pl: the mass of a community as distinguished from a special class ⟨disputes between the ~ and the nobles⟩ — often used by Communists to distinguish Communists or those under Communist control from other people ⟨the People's Court⟩ ⟨Bulgarian People's Republic⟩ **5** pl peoples: a body of persons that are united by a common culture, tradition, or sense of kinship, that typically have common language, institutions, and beliefs, and that often constitute a politically organized group **6**: lower animals usu. of a specified kind or situation ⟨squirrels and chipmunks: the little furry ~⟩ **7**: the body of enfranchised citizens of a state

2people vt peopled; peo·pling \-p(ə-)liŋ\ [MF peupler, fr. OF, fr. peuple] **1**: to supply or fill with people ⟨~ him up⟩ **2**: to dwell in: INHABIT

peo·ple·hood \'pē-pəl-,hud\ n **1**: the quality or state of constituting a people **2**: the awareness of the underlying unity that makes the individual a part of a people

peo·ple·less \'pē-pəl-(l)əs\ adj: void of people

1pep \'pep\ n [short for pepper]: brisk energy or initiative and high spirits

2pep vt pepped; pep·ping: to inject pep into ⟨~ him up⟩

pep·los \'pep-ləs, -,läs\ also **pep·lus** \-ləs\ n [L peplus, fr. Gk peplos]: a garment like a shawl worn by women of ancient Greece

pep·lum \-ləm\ n [L, fr. Gk peplon peplos]: a short section attached to the waistline of a blouse, jacket, or dress — **pep·lumed** \-ləmd\ adj

pe·po \'pē-(,)pō\ n, pl pepos [L, a melon — more at PUMPKIN]: an indehiscent fleshy 1-celled or falsely 3-celled many-seeded berry (as a pumpkin, squash, melon, or cucumber) that has a hard rind and is the characteristic fruit of the gourd family

1pep·per \'pep-ər\ n [ME peper, fr. OE pipor, akin to OHG pfeffar pepper, both fr. a prehistoric WGmc-NGmc word borrowed fr. L piper pepper, fr. Gk peperi] **1 a**: either of two pungent products from the fruit of an East Indian plant that are used as a condiment

molle) of the sumac family grown as a shade tree in mild regions

2pep·per \'pep-(ə-)rē\ adj **1**: of, relating to, or having the qualities of pepper: HOT, PUNGENT ⟨a ~ taste⟩ **2**: having a hot temper: TOUCHY ⟨a ~ boss⟩ **3**: FIERY, STINGING ⟨a ~ satire⟩

pep pill n: any of various stimulant drugs in pill or tablet form

pep·py \'pep-ē\ adj pep·pi·er; -est: full of pep — **pep·pi·ness** n

pep·sin \'pep-sən\ n [G, fr. Gk pepsis digestion, fr. peptein] **1 a**: a proteinase of the stomach that breaks down most proteins to polypeptides **b**: a preparation containing pepsin that is obtained from the stomach esp. of the hog and is used esp. as a digestive

pep·sin·o·gen \pep-'sin-ə-jən\ n [ISV pepsin + -o- + -gen]: a granular zymogen of the gastric glands that is readily converted into pepsin in a slightly acid medium

pep talk n: a usu. brief, high-pressure, and emotional talk designed to influence or encourage an audience

pep·tic \'pep-tik\ adj [L pepticus, fr. Gk peptikos, fr. peptos cooked, fr. peptein, pessein to cook, digest — more at COOK] **1**: relating to or promoting digestion: DIGESTIVE **2**: of, relating to, producing, or caused by pepsin ⟨~ digestion⟩ **3**: connected with or resulting from the action of digestive juices ⟨a ~ ulcer⟩

pep·ti·dase \'pep-tə-,dās, -,dāz\ n: an enzyme that hydrolyzes simple peptides or their derivatives

pep·tide \'pep-,tīd\ n [ISV, fr. peptone]: any of various amides that are derived from two or more amino acids by combination of the amino group of one acid with the carboxyl group of another and are usu. obtained by partial hydrolysis of proteins — **pep·tid·ic** \pep-'tid-ik\ adj — **pep·tid·i·cal·ly** \-i-k(ə-)lē\ adv

peptide bond n: the chemical bond between carbon and nitrogen in a peptide linkage

peptide linkage n: the bivalent group CO–NH that unites the amino acid residues in a peptide

pep·ti·do·gly·can \,pep-təd-ō-'glī-,kan\ n [peptide + -o- + glycan (polysaccharide)]: a polymer that is composed of polysaccharide and peptide chains and is found esp. in bacterial cell walls

pep·tize \'pep-,tīz\ vt pep·tized; pep·tiz·ing [prob. fr. Gk peptein] : to cause to disperse in a medium: specif: to bring into colloidal solution — **pep·ti·za·tion** \,pep-tə-'zā-shən\ n — **pep·tiz·er** \'pep-,tī-zər\ n

pep·tone \'pep-,tōn\ n [G pepton, fr. Gk, neut. of peptos cooked]: any of various water-soluble products of partial hydrolysis of proteins

pep·to·nize \'pep-tə-,nīz\ vt -nized; -niz·ing **1**: to convert into peptone; esp: to digest or dissolve by a proteolytic enzyme **2**: to combine with peptone

Pe·quot \'pē-,kwät\ n [prob. modif. of Narraganset paquatauog destroyers]: a member of an Amerindian people of eastern Connecticut

1per \(')pər\ prep [L, through, by means of, by — more at FOR] **1**: by the means or agency of: THROUGH ⟨~ bearer⟩ **2**: with respect to every member of a specified group: for each **3**: according to ⟨~ list price⟩

2per abbr **1** period **2** person

$C_{11}H_{17}N_2O_2Na$, soluble in water: used in medicine as a sedative, hypnotic, and analgesic

pen·tode (pen′tōd) n.[PENT(A)- + -ODE¹] an electron tube containing five electrodes, usually, a cathode, anode, and three grids: used as a voltage amplifier

☆**pen·tom·ic** (pen täm′ik) adj. [PEN(TA)- + (A)TOMIC] designating or of a military force organized primarily in units of five, esp. for nuclear warfare

pen·to·san (pen′tə san′) n. [PENTOS(E) + -AN] any of a group of plant carbohydrates which form pentoses upon undergoing hydrolysis

pen·tose (pen′tōs) n. [PENT- + -OSE¹] any of a group of monosaccharides having a composition corresponding to the formula $C_5H_{10}O_5$, including ribose, arabinose, etc.

pen·to·side (pen′tə sīd′) n. [PENT(OSE) + (GLYC)OSIDE] a sugar derivative that yields a pentose on hydrolysis

☆**Pen·to·thal Sodium** (-thôl′) [pento- for PENTA- (because of methylbutyl five-carbon group) + thiobarbiturate] + -AL (as in VERONAL, BARBITAL)] a trademark for THIOPENTAL SODIUM: often clipped to **Pentothal**

pent·ox·ide (pen täk′sīd) n. [PENT- + OXIDE] an oxide that contains five oxygen atoms in its molecule

☆**pent·ste·mon** (pent stē′mən, pent′stə-) n. same as PENSTEMON

pent-up (pent′up′) adj. held in check; curbed; confined [pent-up emotion]

pen·tyl (pen′til) n. [PENT(A)- + -YL] same as AMYL

Pen·tyl·ene·tet·ra·zol (pen′tl ēn·tet′rə zôl′, -zōl′) n. [< pent(a-meth)ylene-tetrazol(e)] a white, crystalline powder, $C_6H_{10}N_4$, used as a circulatory and respiratory stimulant and formerly in shock therapy

☆**pe·nu·che, pe·nu·chi** (pə nōō′chē) n. [var. of PANOCHA] a candy resembling fudge, made of brown sugar, milk, butter, and, sometimes, nuts

☆**pe·nuch·le, pe·nuck·le** (pē′nuk′′l) n. same as PINOCHLE

pe·nult (pē′nult, pi nult′) n. [L. paenultima < paene, almost (see PASSION) + ultima, fem. of ultimus, last: see ULTIMATE] the one next to the last; specif., the second last syllable in a word: also **pe·nul′ti·ma** (pi nul′tə mə)

pe·nul·ti·mate (pi nul′tə mit) adj. [< prec., after ULTI-MATE] 1. next to the last 2. of the penult —n. the penult —**pe·nul′ti·mate·ly** adv.

pe·num·bra (pi num′brə) n., pl. -brae (-brē), -bras [ModL. < paene, almost (see PASSION) + umbra, shade] 1. the partly lighted area surrounding the complete shadow of a body, as the moon, in full eclipse: see ECLIPSE, illus. 2. the less dark region surrounding the dark central area of a sunspot 3. a vague, indefinite, or borderline area —pe-

---

particular person or body, as a number of servants, royal subjects, etc. 4. the members of (someone's) class, occupation, set, race, tribe, etc. [the miner spoke for his people] 5. one's relatives or ancestors; family 6. persons without wealth, influence, privilege, or distinction; populace 7. the citizens or electorate of a state 8. persons considered indefinitely [what will people say?] 9. human beings, as distinct from other animals 10. a group of creatures [the ant people] —vt. -pled, -pling [Fr. peupler < the n.] to fill with or as with people; populate; stock

people mover a means of transporting many people over short distances, as a moving sidewalk or an automated monorail

☆**People's party** see POPULIST

Pe·o·ri·a (pē ôr′ē ə) [< Fr. Peouarea, a tribal name < Algonquian piwarea,] he carries a pack] city in C Ill., on the Illinois River: pop. 127,000

☆**pep** (pep) n.[< PEPPER][Colloq.] energy; vigor; liveliness; spirit —vt. pepped, pep′ping [Colloq.] to fill with pep; invigorate; stimulate (with up)

pep·er·o·ni (pep′ə rō′nē) n. same as PEPPERONI

Pep·in the Short (pep′in) 715?-768 A.D.; king of the Franks (751-768): father of CHARLEMAGNE

pep·los (pep′ləs) n. [Gr.] a large shawl or scarf worn draped about the body by women in ancient Greece

pep·lum (pep′ləm) n., pl. -lums, -la (-lə) [L. < Gr. peplos: cf. prec.] 1. orig., a peplos 2. a flounce or short, flared flap attached at the waist of a dress, blouse, coat, etc. and extending around the hips

pe·po (pē′pō) n., pl. -pos [L., species of large melon: see PUMPKIN] any fleshy gourd fruit with a hard rind and many seeds, as the melon, squash, etc.

pep·per (pep′ər) n. see PLURAL, II, D, 3 [ME. peper < OE. pipor < WGmc. borrowing < L. piper < Gr. peperi, via Per. < Sans. pippali, peppercorn] 1. a) a pungent condiment obtained from the small, dried fruits of an East Indian plant (Piper nigrum) of the pepper family: black pepper is ground from the entire fruits, including the fleshy coverings; white pepper, from the internal tissues only b) the plant itself, a vine with smooth, soft stems 2. any of various plants (families Myrtaceae, Zingiberaceae, etc.) possessing aromatic and pungent properties, used in flavoring foods 3. a) same as CAPSICUM b) the fruit of the capsicum: see RED PEPPER, GREEN PEPPER, SWEET PEPPER 4. any of

PEPPER

pe·nu·tri·ous·ly *adv.* —**pe·nu·tri·ous·ness** *n.*

pen·u·ry (pen′yə rē) *n.* [ME. *penurie* < L. *penuria*, want, scarcity < *paene*, scarcely: see PASSION] lack of money, property, or necessities; extreme poverty; destitution —*SYN.* see POVERTY

☆**Pe·nu·ti·an** (pə nōōt′ē ən, pə nōō′shən) *n.* [arbitrary coinage < AmInd. *pen*, two + *uti*, two + -AN] a linguistic phylum or group of remotely related language families in W N. America, including the Chinook, Sahaptin, etc.

Pen·za (pen′zä) city in the SW R.S.F.S.R., southeast of Moscow: pop. 324,000

Pen·zance (pen zans′) city in SW Cornwall, England, on the English Channel: pop. 19,000

pe·on (pē′än, -ən; *for 3, Brit.* pyōōn) *n.* [< Sp. *peón* or (in sense 2) Port. *pedo*, both < ML. *pedo*, foot soldier: see PAWN¹] 1. in Latin America, *a*) a person of the laboring class *b*) formerly, a person forced to work off a debt or to perform penal servitude ☆2. in the SW U.S., formerly, a person forced into servitude to work off a debt 3. in India, *a*) a foot soldier *b*) a native policeman *c*) an attendant or footman 4. an unskilled or exploited laborer

pe·on·age (pē′ə nij) *n.* [see -AGE] 1. the condition of a peon 2. the system by which debtors or legal prisoners are held in servitude to labor for their creditors or for persons who lease their services from the state

pe·o·ny (pē′ə nē) *n., pl.* -**nies** [ME. *pione* < OE. *peonie &* OFr. *peone*, both < L. *paeonia* < Gr. *paiōnia* < *Paiōn*, epithet of Apollo, physician of the gods: from its former medicinal use] 1. any of a genus (*Paeonia*) of perennial, often double-flowered, plants of the buttercup family, with large pink, white, red, or yellow, showy flowers 2. the flower

peo·ple (pē′p'l) *n., pl.* -**ple**; *for 1 & 10*, -**ples** [ME. *peple* < Anglo-Fr. *people, people* < OFr. *pople* < L. *populus*, nation, crowd < ?] 1. *a*) all the persons of a racial, national, religious, or linguistic group; nation, race, etc. (*the peoples of the world*) *b*) a group of persons with common traditional, historical, or cultural ties, as distinct from racial or political unity (*the Jewish people*) 2. the persons belonging to a certain place, community, or class (*the people of Iowa, people of wealth*) 3. the members of a group under the leadership, influence, or control of a

(... [top cut off] ...) of plants, including cubeb and pepper (4. 1 *b*) —*vt.* 1. to sprinkle or flavor with ground pepper 2. to sprinkle freely or thickly 3. to shower or pelt with many small objects (*a roof peppered with hailstones*) 4. to beat or hit with short, quick jabs

pep·per-and-salt (-'n sôlt′) *adj.* dotted or speckled with contrasting colors, esp. black and white

pep·per·box (-bäks′) *n. same as* PEPPER SHAKER

pep·per·corn (-kôrn′) *n.* [ME. *pepercorn* < OE. *piporcorn*] 1. the dried berry of the black PEPPER (*n.* 1) 2. something insignificant or trifling

pep·per·grass (-gras′, -gräs′) *n.* any of a genus (*Lepidium*) of small plants of the mustard family, with small whitish flowers and flattened pods; esp., *same as* GARDEN CRESS

pep·per·idge (-ij) *n.* [var. of Brit. dial. *pipperidge*, the barberry] *same as* BLACK GUM

pep·per·mill a hand mill used to grind peppercorns

pep·per·mint (-mint′, -mənt) *n.* 1. an aromatic, perennial plant (*Mentha piperita*) of the mint family, with lance-shaped leaves and whitish or purplish flowers in dense terminal spikes 2. the pungent oil it yields, used for flavoring 3. a candy or lozenge flavored with this oil

☆**pep·per·o·ni** (pep′ə rō′nē) *n., pl.* -**nis, -ni** [< It. *peperoni*, pl. of *peperone*, cayenne peppers] a hard, highly spiced Italian sausage

pepper pot 1. *same as* PEPPER SHAKER 2. a West Indian stew of vegetables and meat or fish, flavored with cassava juice, red pepper, etc. ☆3. a hotly seasoned stew of vegetables, dumplings, tripe, etc. 4. a soup of meat and vegetables flavored with hot spices

pepper shaker a container with a perforated top, for sprinkling ground pepper

pepper tree a S. American ornamental tree (*Schinus molle*) of the cashew family, with panicles of yellowish flowers, pinnately compound leaves, and pinkish-red berries

pep·per·wort (-wurt′) *n.* 1. *same as* PEPPERGRASS 2. any of a genus (*Marsilea*) of water ferns having long-stalked leaves with four leaflets

pep·per·y (-ē) *adj.* 1. of, like, or highly seasoned with pepper 2. sharp or fiery, as speech or writing 3. hot tempered; irritable —**pep′per·i·ness** *n.*

☆**pep pill** [Slang] any of various pills or tablets containing a stimulant, esp. amphetamine

fat, āpe, cär; ten, ēven; is, bīte; gō, hôrn, tōōl, look; oil, out; up, fur; get; joy; yet; chin; she; thin, *then*; zh, leisure; ŋ, ring; ə for *a* in *ago*, *e* in *agent*, *i* in *sanity*, *o* in *comply*, *u* in *focus*; ' as in *able* (ā′b'l); Fr. bal; ë, Fr. cœur; ö, Fr. feu; Fr. mon; ü, Fr. coq; ɧ, Fr. duc; r̃, Fr. cri; H, G. ich; kh, G. doch. See inside front cover. ☆ Americanism; ‡ foreign; * hypothetical; < derived from

life." I recently saw the *seventh* edition of *Webster's* with a shiny new cover, right up front in a dictionary section as if it were new on the market. You won't get salmonellosis from the seventh *Webster's*, but you'll get plenty of frustration. While yet to be proven in use, *Webster's Ninth* makes two changes from its predecessor that are of special interest to learners. One is that it includes in its definitions, when possible, the date of a word's first use. This fact is not as valuable as the more extensive sort of etymological information, and certainly questionable in terms of verification, but it is an interesting and unique addition to the material usually found in collegiate dictionary definitions and does represent greater attention to etymology on the part of the collegiate *Webster's*. The other improvement is that *Webster's Ninth* pays more attention to usage level. In terms of front matter and clarity of definition, the new dictionary remains largely the same; unfortunately, its design has gotten even more cramped.

Webster's New World—the "other" *Webster's*—is a rival in more than name. It has a more comfortable typeface than *Webster's New Collegiate*, but, besides its relative deficiency in illustrations, it does not employ as many typographical aids as *American Heritage* for discrimination, nor does it offer as much space. Particularly, its prefatory material is set in very small type. Although *Webster's New World* has no connection with the Merriam-Webster company that publishes *Webster's New Collegiate*, and is not derived from an unabridged dictionary, its definitions have been acclaimed by reference authorities and prestigious publications as the best in any of the dictionaries reviewed here. One strength is its special coverage of Americanisms. A drawback in clarity of definition, however, is that it uses only staff-written phrases for illustration. It is strong on etymology in general. As for usage level, it offers a compromise between *American Heritage* and *Webster's New Collegiate*. It does not, however, have front matter the equal of either of these.

A few warnings are in order. Although many people have heard that *The OED—The Oxford English Dictionary*—is the dictionary to beat all dictionaries (and it is) it is not really suited for general purposes. In some sources, *The American College Dictionary*, once published by Random House, is still recom-

mended for college use. When it came out during the '40s it was regarded as highly authoritative and among its other achievements, it pioneered an emphasis on Americanisms. It was kept current through the '60s, but Random House has now let it go out of print.

"The sweetest path of life leads through the avenues of learning," wrote David Hume, an eighteenth-century Scottish philosopher whose views were seldom so saccharine. Even if the path turns rough, you may find sweetness along the way with the best of learning tools, a good dictionary.

Sample Questions for Dictionaries

1. Which usage is correct: "different from" or "different than"?

2. Where is the parietal lobe of the brain located?

3. If I had lived in Chaucer's time, would I have been able to understand the English that people spoke then?

4. Does "humble" come from the same root as "human"?

5. What is the "Golden Rule"?

6. What does "sympatric" mean and does it have too specialized a meaning to use in my history paper?

7. What does the word "anathema" mean and where can I find an example of its use?

8. I recently saw the word "sourdough" applied to a person, but I thought "sourdough" was a kind of bread. Where does the other usage come from?

9. How deep is a fathom?

10. Does "teddy bear" really have anything to do with Theodore Roosevelt? What's the connection?

THESAURUS

2. SYNONYM BOOKS

To dance with the body, with ideas, with words . . .

Loosely translated from Friedrich Wilheim
Nietzsche (1844–1900)

A synonym book, or synonymy, should stand right next to your dictionary. It will extend your use of the dictionary to help you explore a word's meaning because it will tell you the words most closely associated with it or, on the other hand, words with the opposite sense. When you use a synonymy to pursue meaning, you are a little like a witness who gets closer and closer to identifying a criminal by looking at a series of artist's sketches. Paradoxically, this process of narrowing is also enlarging. The witness is increasingly seeing the criminal as part of a physiological group to which s/he belongs—a unifying shape—and the learner is getting to know a family of meanings to which a word is related—a root concept. Looking up a synonym, then, is seldom a trivial job; it can often be a guide for thought, or it can be a way of getting the thought process started in the first place.

The other use for a synonymy is to give your diction some life. In many cases, it can encourage you to find a specific word to replace a general one: you may look up "colorful" and be led to hundreds of vivid shades, from "apricot" to "cochineal." And it can always provide variety. If you've used the word "significant" six times on one page and are getting bored with it, you can find other words to substitute: the obvious "important," "notable," or "meaningful," even "striking,"

"weighty," "telling," not to mention "trenchant," "pithy," or "pregnant." Naturally, you should only tinker with your prose in this way after you've gotten the ideas down straight— changes in wording that may enhance a strong point may muddle a weak one. Also, you must be sensitive to levels of diction so that you do not inadvertently replace, say, an informal word with a formal one and puzzle readers with the shift. Finally, you need to work back and forth with the dictionary at times when you are not familiar with a substitute word. Learners who try to enlarge their vocabularies artificially with a synonym book often come out with sentences as awkward as dubbed-in sound. If humor is intended, these con's turn into pro's (witness the delightful slang version of "The Declaration of Independence").

Once you set out to buy a synonymy, you will find they take up more space on bookstore shelves these days than dictionaries do. Perhaps they are proliferating so rapidly because they can be abbreviated more easily than dictionaries. This section of the book reviews a sample of the synonymies most commonly sold to learners. They are not all as similar as their covers make them seem.

You can tell synonymies apart by their approaches. One approach is to discriminate between words that are almost identical in meaning with a given word, but different in usage. This type of synonomy assumes you want correction in your choice of words and so limits the horizons. Another approach is to collect as many words as possible that have more or less overlapping meanings with a given word or, in the case of a general word, that are specifics for it. This type of synonomy assumes you want suggestions, and so tosses lots of words in widening circles of relatedness around a given word, leading you on. The first type of synonymy must, by definition, provide discriminatory essays. The second type does not, it simply supplies word lists. The labels "dictionary of discriminated synonyms" and "thesaurus" help distinguish the two, since the first explicitly mentions discrimination, while thesaurus means "treasurehouse." While, unfortunately, these labels have not seen much use, even by experts, they will be used below.

Other approaches are represented below by dictionaries of

*un*discriminated synonyms, which make speed their highest priority, and by hybrids or different kinds of synonymies altogether. Titles are listed in order of preference within the first three categories and alphabetically within the last.

Thesauri

Pure thesauri are not for the lazy. They are hard to use, since you must first consult the front or the back of the book for the word at hand and then turn to other pages to find its synonyms and antonyms. They are also dangerous to use, since they do not provide any definitions beyond the most rudimentary that serve as the index, and they offer little guidance on usage. Yet no other synonymy is as expansive and free as a thesaurus. That is so because no other synonymy is organized solely by word *meaning*.

The key to the thesaurus's organization is found in the synopsis of categories at the front of the book. There, all the ideas or things that words can express are divided into several classes: "abstract relations," for instance, or "volition," or "matter"; under which may be found, respectively, "order," "custom," or "organic matter," and so on through two more levels of subheadings. This taxonomy of concepts not only is exhilarating for its breadth, but helps guide you efficiently to possible words for a given thought without narrowing the scope of choice too quickly or too rigidly. Alternatively, you can find a specific word in the index at the back of the book and follow directions from there to synonyms. In a thesaurus, for instance, the synonyms for "fad" are not found listed near those words with similar spelling—between those for "faculty" and "fade"—they are found near others that are related in meaning, that is, under the heading of "fashion," which in turn falls under a more general heading of "custom," a part of "volition," as mentioned above. Moreover, the more general headings under which words are arranged go in order of contrasted meaning; thus, to find the antonym for "fad" you look from "fashion" to the nearby heading of "unaccustomedness." Turn by turn, a thread is constantly unwound from vocabulary to the structure of thought. This type of synonymy can

turn a mechanical chore into an intellectual adventure. For understanding words better (as opposed to manipulating them more gracefully), the thesaurus is a unique aid. Indeed, it is the synonymy that best embodies the spirit of liberal education.

Chapman, Robert L., ed. *Roget's International Thesaurus*. 4th edition. New York: Thomas Y. Crowell, 1977. 1317 pp.

> Bear in mind that the name "Roget" is not a trademark and so appears in many titles of synonymies. By itself, it is no guide to quality. This title is the "classic" *Roget*. It is reasonably up-to-date and intelligently revised from its ancestor, the thesaurus begun in 1852 by Dr. Peter Roget. It continues to be the most authoritative among its endangered species.

Dutch, Robert A., ed. *The St. Martin's Roget's Thesaurus of English Words and Phrases*. New York: St. Martin's, 1965. 1405 pp.

> This is better than *Roget's International* for the American user because it stresses American slang and colloquial words. Also, there has been an effort to improve on its chief rival's categorization of meanings. Its main drawback is that it is less current than the fourth *Roget's International*. Nonetheless, it is an excellent thesaurus.

Mawson, C. O. Sylvester, ed. *Roget's Pocket Thesaurus*. New York: Pocket Books, 1976. 484 pp.

> A reprinted paperback edition of an old *Roget's International*, it has a light but cogent Introduction by I. A. Richards that is worth preserving in and of itself. Otherwise, it suffers from abbreviations, and the edition on which it is based, with only slight revisions, is from 1922.

Dictionaries of Discriminated Synonyms

Figuratively speaking, "dictionary of discriminated synonyms" is the antonym for "thesaurus." This type of synonymy is not for the lazy either, however. Painstakingly teasing out individual threads of meaning from tangles of seeming synonyms, it is indispensable for any thinking or writing task where precision is paramount. Even more than a dictionary, this type of synonymy reinforces the spirit of correctness and propriety in language. It is a profoundly conservative and reassuring reference tool.

Gove, Philip B., ed. *Webster's New Dictionary of Synonyms.* Springfield, Mass.: Merriam-Webster, 1980. 942 pp.

The authors of this work affirm the importance of this type of synonymy, yet they acknowledge the advantages of a thesaurus by adding to the discriminatory essay on each word a list of analogous or contrasted words. In short, they try to sneak in the work of both types. Because of its thorough essays and the authoritativeness of the vocabulary from which it draws (*Webster's Third*), *Webster's New Dictionary of Synonyms* is a model of its type. Its extensive use of illustrative quotations is helpful and appealing.

Hayakawa, S. I., ed. *Funk & Wagnalls Modern Guide to Synonyms.* New York: Funk & Wagnalls, 1968. 726 pp.

The essays in this volume are on a par with those in the preceding one, and some critics have found them more readable. Certainly, any editorial job predominantly associated with one writer will have more style. *Funk & Wagnalls* is also more attractive graphically and easier to read than *Webster's*. However, it does not marshal as many illustrative quotations, is not as recent, and covers far fewer words.

644. FASHION

.1 NOUNS **fashion, style, mode, vogue,** trend, prevailing taste; proper thing; *bon ton* [Fr], custom 642; convention 645.1,2; swim [informal], current or stream of fashion; height of fashion; the new look, the season's look; high fashion, *haute couture* [Fr].

.2 **fashionableness,** *bon ton* [Fr], fashionability, **stylishness, modishness,** voguishness; **popularity,** prevalence, currency 79.2.

.3 **smartness, chic, elegance;** style-consciousness, clothes-consciousness; **spruceness, nattiness,** neatness, trimness, sleekness, **dapperness,** jauntiness; sharpness or spiffiness or classiness or niftiness [all slang]; swankness or swankiness [both informal]; foppery, foppishness, coxcombry, dandyism.

.4 **the rage, the thing, the last word** [informal], *le dernier cri* [Fr], **the latest thing,** the latest wrinkle [informal].

.5 **fad, craze, rage;** wrinkle [informal]; novelty 122.2; faddishness, faddiness [informal], faddism; **faddist.**

.6 **society,** *société* [Fr], fashionable society,

.10 **follow the fashion, get in the swim** [informal], get or jump on the bandwagon [slang], join the parade, follow the crowd, go with the stream or tide or current; keep in step, do as others do; keep up, **keep up appearances,** keep up with the Joneses.

.11 ADJS **fashionable, in fashion, smart, in style, in vogue; all the rage,** all the thing; **popular,** prevalent, current 79.12; **up-to-date,** up-to-datish, up-to-the-minute, hip or mod [both slang], trendy [informal], newfashioned, modern, new 122.9–14; in **the swim.**

.12 **stylish, modish,** voguish, vogue; soigné or soignée [both Fr]; *à la mode* [Fr], in the mode.

.13 **chic, smart,** elegant; style-conscious, clothes-conscious; **well-dressed,** well-groomed, *soigné* or *soignée* [both Fr], dressed to advantage, dressed to kill, dressed to the teeth, dressed to the nines, well-turned-out; **spruce, natty,** neat, trim, sleek, smug, trig, tricksy [archaic]; **dapper,** dashing, jaunty, braw [Scot]; sharp or spiffy or classy or nifty or snazzy [all slang]; **swank** or **swanky** [both informal], posh [informal], ritzy [informal], swell or

.14 **ultrafashionable,** ultrastylish, ultrasmart; chichi; foppish, dandified, dandyish, dandiacal.

.15 **faddish, faddy** [informal].

.16 **socially prominent,** in society, high-society, elite; café-society, jet-set; lace-curtain, silk-stocking.

.17 ADVS **fashionably, stylishly, modishly,** *à la mode* [Fr], in the latest style or mode.

.18 **smartly,** chicly, elegantly, exquisitely; **sprucely, nattily,** neatly, trimly, sleekly; **dapperly,** jauntily, dashingly, swankly or swankily [both informal]; foppishly, dandyishly.

645. SOCIAL CONVENTION

.1 NOUNS **social convention,** convention, conventional usage, social usage, form, **formality; custom** 642; conformity 82; propriety, decorum, decorousness, correctness, *convenance, bienséance* [both Fr], decency, seemliness, civility [archaic], good form, etiquette 646.3; **conventionalism,** conventionality, Grundyism; Mrs. Grundy.

.2 **the conventions, the proprieties, the mores,** the right things, accepted or sanc-

---

ion, right people; best people, people of fashion; *monde* [Fr], world of fashion, Vanity Fair, **smart set** [informal]; the Four Hundred, **upper crust** or **upper cut** [both informal]; **cream of society,** elite, carriage trade; café society, jet set, beautiful people, in-crowd; *jeunesse dorée* [Fr]; drawing room, salon; social register.

.7 **person of fashion,** fashionable, man-about-town, man or woman of the world, *mondain, mondaine* [both Fr], leader or arbiter of fashion, taste-maker, trend-setter, tone-setter, *arbiter elegantiae* [L]; ten best-dressed, fashion plate, clotheshorse, "the glass of fashion and the mold of form" [Shakespeare], Beau Brummel; fop, dandy 903.9; **socialite** [informal]; **clubwoman,** clubman; jet setter; swinger [informal]; **debutante,** subdebutante, deb or subdeb [both informal].

.8 VERBS **catch on,** become popular, **become the rage.**

.9 **be fashionable, be the style, be the rage,** be the thing; have a run; cut a figure in society [informal]; give a tone to society; set the fashion or style or tone; dress to kill.

factor 1 *agent, attorney, deputy, proxy
2 constituent, *element, component, ingredient
Ana determinant, *cause, antecedent: *influence: agency, agent, instrument, instrumentality, *mean

faculty 1 *power, function
2 *gift, aptitude, knack, bent, turn, genius, talent
Ana *ability, capacity, capability: property, *quality: penchant, flair, propensity, proclivity, *leaning: *predilection

fad vogue, *fashion, style, rage, craze, mode, dernier cri, cry
Ana fancy, whim, whimsy, *caprice, conceit, vagary

fade *vanish, evanesce, evaporate, disappear
Ana deliquesce, melt (see LIQUEFY): *thin, rarefy, attenuate: reduce, lessen (see DECREASE)

faded *shabby, dilapidated, dingy, seedy, threadbare
Ana worn, wasted, *haggard: dim, murky, gloomy (see DARK): *colorless, achromatic: *pale, pallid, ashen, wan

fag *vb* exhaust, jade, fatigue, *tire, weary, tucker

failing *n* frailty, foible, *fault, vice
Ana *blemish, flaw, defect: weakness, infirmity (see corresponding adjectives at WEAK)
Ant perfection (*in concrete sense*) —*Con* *excellence, merit, virtue

failure, neglect, default, miscarriage, dereliction are comparable when they mean an omission on the part of someone or something of what is expected or required of him or of it. **Failure** basically implies a being found wanting; it implies a lack or absence of something that might have been expected to occur or to be accomplished, performed, or effected ⟨there was a general *failure* of crops that year⟩ ⟨a distressing confusion in discussions of the human-interest story has been caused by a common *failure* to define the term—*Mott*⟩ ⟨you will hear a great some *miscarriage* in the details of our plan—*Krutch*⟩ ⟨these various *miscarriages* cannot all be ascribed to ill fortune—*Grenfell*⟩ **Dereliction,** of all these terms, carries the strongest implication of a neglect that amounts to an abandonment of, or a departure from, the thing and especially the duty, the principle, or the law that should have been uppermost in a person's mind; ordinarily it implies a morally reprehensible failure rather than one resulting from carelessness and inattention or from mishap ⟨they would be answerable with their lives for any further *dereliction* of duty—*Ainsworth*⟩ ⟨it revealed in him . . . the indisputable signs of a certain *dereliction* from some path of development his nature had commanded him to follow—*Brooks*⟩
Ana *fault, failing: shortcoming, deficiency, *imperfection: *lack, want, absence, privation, dearth: negligence, laxness, slackness, remissness (see corresponding adjectives at NEGLIGENT): indifference, unconcernedness *or* unconcern (see corresponding adjectives at INDIFFERENT)

fainéant *adj* indolent, slothful, *lazy
Ana supine, passive, *inactive, inert, idle: apathetic, *impassive, phlegmatic: *lethargic, sluggish: languorous, lackadaisical, *languid

fair *adj* 1 comely, lovely, *beautiful, pretty, bonny, handsome, beauteous, pulchritudinous, good-looking
Ana delicate, dainty, exquisite (see CHOICE): charming, attractive, enchanting (see under ATTRACT): pure, *chaste
Ant foul: ill-favored
2 **Fair, just, equitable, impartial, unbiased, dispassionate, uncolored, objective** are comparable when they are applied to judgments or to judges or to acts resulting from or involving a judgment and mean free from undue or improper influence. **Fair,** the most general term, implies

Neglect (see also NEGLIGENCE) implies carelessness and inattentiveness on the part of a person, so that what is expected or required of him is either left unattended to or is not adequately performed ⟨in wartime a charge of *neglect* of duty is a very serious one⟩ ⟨his *neglect* of his health is a source of much worry to his friends⟩ ⟨the property has become dilapidated through the owner's *neglect*⟩ ⟨we made a nice tidy cleanup . . . If I hadn't done it I ought . . . to have been shot for *neglect*—H. G. Wells⟩ Default is now chiefly found in legal use, where it implies a failure to perform something required by law (as a failure of a plaintiff or of a defendant to appear at the appointed time to prosecute or defend an action or a proceeding) ⟨in case of *default* on the part of the plaintiff, he may be nonsuited⟩ ⟨in case of *default* on the part of the defendant, he may have a judgment rendered against him, this being called a *judgment by default*⟩ *Default* may also imply a failure to pay one's debts at the appointed time ⟨convicted of *default* in the payment of a fine⟩ or in extended use a failure to perform something required, usually by total omission of pertinent action ⟨betraying by *default* the privileges of citizenship in a democratic society—*Dean*⟩ ⟨lose a tennis match by *default*⟩ Miscarriage does not so definitely point the blame for a failure of someone or something to live up to expectations or to accomplish certain ends as do the preceding words: it is often used when there are no definite persons or things to which culpability can be assigned or when for some reason or other there is a serious desire to avoid casting of blame ⟨there was a serious *miscarriage* of justice in that trial⟩ ⟨the causes of the *miscarriage* of the project were not clear⟩ ⟨we fear . . .

Ana analogous words   *Ant* antonyms   *Con* contrasted words

reasonable claim of the weaker side or of giving oneself or the stronger side no undue advantage ⟨a *fair* distribution of one's estate⟩ ⟨a *fair* decision by a judge⟩ ⟨*fair* play⟩ ⟨when we consider how helpless a partridge is . . . it does seem *fairer* that the gunner should have but one chance at the bird—*Jefferies*⟩ ⟨I believe you will find them a *fair* solution of this complicated and difficult problem—*Roosevelt*⟩ Just implies no divergence from the standard or measure of what has been determined or is accepted as right, true, or lawful and dealings that are exactly in accordance with those determinations, no matter what one's personal inclinations or interests may be or what considerations in favor of the person or thing judged may be adduced ⟨a *just* judge⟩ ⟨some *juster* prince perhaps had . . . safe restored me to my native land—*Pope*⟩ ⟨how much easier it is to be generous than *just*—*Junius*⟩ ⟨to divert interest from the poet to the poetry . . . would conduce to a *juster* estimation of actual poetry, good and bad—*T. S. Eliot*⟩ Equitable implies a freer and less rigid standard than *just*, often the one which guides a court of equity as distinguished from a court of law and which provides relief where rigid adherence to the law would make for unfairness ⟨he has an *equitable* claim to the property⟩ More often the word implies fair and equal treatment of all concerned ⟨a form of society which will provide for an *equitable* distribution of . . . riches—*Krutch*⟩ ⟨it depended wholly on their individual characters whether their terms of office were *equitable* or oppressive—*Buchan*⟩ Impartial implies absence of favor for or absence of prejudice against one person, party, or side more than the other ⟨an *impartial* tribunal⟩ ⟨impartial . . .

See also explanatory notes facing page 1

Merriam-Webster Pocket Dictionary of Synonyms. New York: Pocket Books, 1972. 441 pp.

A pocket paperback version of *Webster's New Dictionary of Synonyms*, this is up-to-date and reasonably thorough. It is regarded as one of the best pocket synonym dictionaries.

Dictionaries of Undiscriminated Synonyms

Although many synonymies of this type are called thesauri, they are not at all like the "pure" thesauri described in this chapter because they are organized alphabetically, like dictionaries. In the sense that speed of use has taken precedence over understanding, these synonymies may be called "degenerate." Like thesauri, they provide simply word lists, and do not emphasize definitions.

Kay, Mairé W., ed. *Webster's Collegiate Thesaurus.* Springfield, Mass.: Merriam-Webster, 1976. 944 pp.

This book emphasizes definitions more than any others in this category. It goes beyond word lists but lacks the definitiveness of *Webster's New Dictionary of Synonyms*. Its main virtue is that it is fast to use . . . "instant words," as one bit of ad copy goes. It is also authoritative.

Urdang, Laurence, rev. *Synonym Finder.* Emmaus, Pa.: Rodale, 1978. 1361 pp.

If you want quantity, this book piles the words higher than any other.

Landau, Sidney I., and Ronald J. Bogus, eds. *The Doubleday Roget's Thesaurus of the American Language in Dictionary Form.* Garden City, N.Y.: Doubleday, 1977. 804 pp.

This is comparable to *Webster's Collegiate The-saurus*. Of the two, *Doubleday* has slightly fewer main entries and provides less discriminatory material.

Gilman, E. Ward, ed. *Merriam-Webster Thesaurus*. New York: Pocket Books, 1979. 634 pp.

This is the paperback version of *Webster's Collegiate Thesaurus*.

Laird, Charlton, ed. *Webster's New World Thesaurus*. New York: Simon & Schuster, 1971. 678 pp.

This book is worth respecting because of the excellence of *Webster's New World Dictionary*, on which it is based. Also, Charlton Laird's Introduction would be an asset to any synonymy.

Lewis, Norman, rev. *The New Roget's Thesaurus in Dictionary Form*. New York: G. P. Putnam's Sons, 1978. 496 pp.

This work has not been revised extensively enough since its first publication in 1961 to be authoritative or up-to-date.

Morehead, Philip D., ed. *The New American Roget's Thesaurus in Dictionary Form*. Rev. ed. New York: New American Library, 1978. 572 pp.

This paperback is based on an out-of-date source and is not notably comprehensive.

Other

Bernstein, Theodore M., ed. *Bernstein's Reverse Dictionary*. New York: Times Books, 1975. 276 pp.

Bernstein's is a delightful new tool that can double

3. staff, teacher, schoolmasters, (*chiefly Brit.* masters, (*in the English universities*) dons, instructors, coaches, tutors, academics; professors, professorate, professoriate, academician, lecturers, pedagogues.

4. profession, occupation, vocation, calling, metier; discipline, area, field, branch.

5. power, prerogative, license, right, privilege; permission, authorization, sanction.

fad, *n.* vogue, fashion, style, trend, ton, mode, *Inf.* last word, *Fr.* dernier cri, *Sl.* the thing, *Sl.* latest or newest thing; craze, mania, rage, furor; whim, fancy, crotchet.

fade, *v.* **1.** blanch, blench, bleach, pale, whiten, gray, wash out; dim, cloud, grow dull, lose luster *or* brightness; etiolate, achromatize, decolor, decolorize.

2. languish, waste away, *Dial.* dwine, droop, flag, sag, faint; wither, wilt, shrivel, decay, molder, rot; decline, wane, ebb, fall off; fail, deteriorate, degenerate.

3. dissolve, melt away, deliquesce; disappear, evanesce, vanish, melt into thin air, leave no trace, perish, die.

4. lessen, abate, diminish, decrease, slacken; subside, let up, intermit, cease; taper off, drop off, obsolesce, die out.

fag, *v.* **1.** tire, tire out, exhaust, weary, jade; fatigue, prostrate, *Inf.* tucker out, wear out, knock out, *Sl.* poop, do in; spend, strain, droop, flag.

—*n.* **2.** menial, slave, flunky, *Inf.* gofer; drudge, plodder, moiler, laborer.

3. *Slang.* homosexual. See **homosexual** (*def. 2*).

4. *Slang.* cigarette, *Inf.* butt. See **cigarette.**

fagot, *n.* **1.** bundle of sticks, firewood, kindling; branches, twigs, fascine.

2. bundle, *Sl.* bindle, bale; bunch, cluster; pack,

Pathol. asthenia, *Pathol.* cachexia.

failure, *n.* **1.** lack of success, nonsuccess, nonfulfillment, defeat, frustration, inefficacy; mishap, misfortune, mischance; miscarriage, abortion; blunder, error, slip, trip, stumble, faux pas; botch, muff, mess, muddle; fizzle, fiasco, *Inf.* washout; vain attempt, wild-goose chase, sleeveless errand; checkmate, deathblow, tragedy, debacle, sinking ship; rebuff, repulse, overthrow, discomfiture, beating, drubbing, *Inf.* body blow.

2. delinquency, dereliction, negligence, inadvertency; nonobservance, omission, default, oversight, pretermission; indiscretion, peccadillo, mistake; recreancy, backsliding, apostasy.

3. insufficiency, deficiency, want, lack, dearth, scarcity.

4. deterioration, decline, decay, wasting away, failing, languor, debilitation; collapse, decrepitude, *Pathol.* atony, *Pathol.* asthenia, *Pathol.* cachexia.

5. bankruptcy, insolvency, financial disaster; crash, wreck, ruination, downfall.

6. unsuccessful person *or* thing, also-ran, lead balloon, *Inf.* flop, *Sl.* bomb, *Sl.* brodie, *Inf.* clunker, *Inf.* lemon, *Inf.* dud, *Sl.* clinker, *Inf.* bummer, *Sl.* bust; down-and-outer, loser, schlemiel, *Sl.* dog.

faint, *adj.* **1.** pale, dim, distant, obscure, faded, weak, feeble, thin, faltering, trembling; low, soft, gentle, dulcet, whispered, muted, stifled, muffled; dull, indistinct, unclear, inaudible, imperceptible.

2. dizzy, *Inf.* woozy, vertiginous, lightheaded, giddy; weak, exhausted, tired, worn out, limp, drooping, about to drop.

3. cowardly, timorous, timid, fearful, afraid, frightened, afraid of one's shadow; unmanly, faint-hearted,

stumble, blunder; shipwreck, run aground, come to grief, meet with disaster, *Inf.* come a cropper; miss the mark, miss the boat, *Sl.* blow it, *Sl.* flush it, *Sl.* bomb, *Sl.* lay an egg, *Sl.* strike out, wash out, labor in vain, come to nothing; fizzle, fink out, *Inf.* flop, *Sl.* bite the dust, lose the day, end in smoke, fall flat, go to wrack and ruin, have had it.

2. fall short, stop short of, not reach, fall by the wayside; be deficient, be insufficient, be defective, be wanting, be lacking; not pass muster, not make the grade, *Sl.* not cut the mustard, flunk; disappoint, prove inadequate, turn out badly.

3. dwindle, decline, decay, deteriorate; pine away, languish, fade away, disappear, cease, pass away; wane, give out, droop, ebb, sink, collapse; sicken, weaken, flag, lose vigor, crumble, be on the ropes, *Sl.* be on the downslide, be on one's last legs.

4. go out of business, go bankrupt, go under, *Inf.* fold *or* fold up, close down, drown in red ink, go to smash, default on payment, not pay.

5. forsake, desert, omit to perform, neglect to observe; ignore, slight, evade, cut, give the go-by to, shut one's eyes to; avoid, escape, renounce, forswear.

failing, *n.* 1. failure, nonsuccess, nonfulfillment; miscarriage, abortion; no-go, vain attempt; fizzle, fiasco, botch, blunder, washout, flash in the pan.

2. shortcoming, fault, imperfection, defect, weakness; frailty, foible, flaw, blemish, infirmity, blind side.

3. delinquency, dereliction, negligence, inadvertency, omission; indiscretion, offense, peccadillo, mistake, slip, error; recreancy, backsliding, apostasy.

4. wasting away, languor, decline, decay, deterioration, debilitation; collapse, decrepitude, *Pathol.* atony

out, *Pathol.* suffer syncope; limpen, go limp, crumple, succumb, give way, keel over, drop, collapse, *Sl.* conk out, die, faint dead away.

5. grow weak, lose strength, languish, droop, fade, flag, diminish, fall off; fail, decline, go downhill, sink. —*n.* 6. unconsciousness, blackout, swoon, fainting spell, *Pathol.* syncope, *Chiefly Scot.* dwalm.

fair[1], *adj.* 1. unbiased, unprejudiced, impartial, uncolored; disinterested, dispassionate, detached; even-handed, equitable, just, *Inf.* square, objective.

2. proper, legitimate, straightforward, aboveboard.

3. ample, sufficient, adequate, OK, enough; moderate, middling, so-so, *Fr. comme ci, comme ça,* indifferent; mediocre, ordinary, common, pretty good, not bad; decent, goodish; passable, tolerable, respectable, reasonable, satisfactory.

4. sunny, bright, cloudless, clear, pleasant; fine, calm, halcyon.

5. unblemished, untarnished, spotless, unstained; impeccable, pure, good, clean, virtuous.

6. blonde, blondish, light brown, pale; creamy, peaches-and-cream, strawberry-blonde.

7. good-looking, comely, pretty, bonny, attractive, well-favored, lovely; beautiful, *Chiefly Literary.* beauteous, pulchritudinous, handsome; dainty, delicate; charming, sweet, enchanting.

8. courteous, gracious, polite, civil, fair-spoken; affable, friendly, agreeable, personable; civilized, suave.

fair[2], *n.* 1. exhibition, show, showing, display, exhibit; livestock show, farm show, horse show; county fair, state fair, harvest fair, country fair, 4-H fair, Grange fair, exposition, *Inf.* expo.

2. market, mart, flea market, bazaar, exchange,

as a dictionary of undiscriminated synonyms, but is much more restricted than other dictionaries of undiscriminated synonyms. Its innovation is to make the *meaning* of a target word the main entry, instead of the target word itself. Bernstein says the need for a reverse dictionary dawned on him at a dinner party when he was trying to think of the word that means "reads the same backwards or forwards," like "madam" or "radar." (Target word: "palindrome.") Can't everyone remember similar puzzles? "What is that fancy foreign word for good feelings people in groups have for each other?" (Target word: "camaraderie.") The main problem with the reverse dictionary is that the word-meaning entry may be just as elusive as the word itself. Would you look for "camaraderie" under "fellowship" (correct), "cooperation," "good-feeling," "brotherhood" (all wrong), or what? The reverse dictionary is not big enough to provide all the logical cross-references, so too often the user is out of luck.

Cousins, Norman, ed. *March's Thesaurus and Dictionary of the English Language*. Rev. and exp. ed. New supplement by Goodwin, R. A., and Stuart B. Flexner. New York: Abbeville, 1980. 1324 pp.

True to its title, this is a combination of a dictionary and a thesaurus. It works the way a dictionary of undiscriminated synonyms does, except that when it comes to a word that identifies a large category of meaning, such as "giving," it breaks into thesaurus form, devoting part of the page, in a box-like arrangement, to word lists under the heading "giving–receiving." Unlike those in a thesaurus, however, its word lists include definitions ("dispensation–divine giving") and so the dictionary aspect of the book is strengthened. This sort of hybrid cannot offer as much as a dictionary, a dictionary of discriminated synonyms, or a thesaurus can offer separately, either in quantity or in quality. One

advantage *March's* has over other synonymies, though, is its supplement, which includes more scientific or technical entries ("Doppler effect," "ABM") than its rivals. It claims as well to include more current sociological terms ("rap," "sexist") but this is harder to substantiate. It also adds categories of meaning in the scientific, technical, and sociological fields to the categories employed by other thesauri. Since the supplement is not fully integrated with the main text, however (even though cross-references are made), it loses much of its appeal for the user, who, in the interest of speed, is willing to accept the basic compromise it represents.

Reader's Digest Family Word Finder: A New Thesaurus of Synonyms and Antonyms in Dictionary Form. Compiled by the *Reader's Digest* editors, in association with Stuart B. Flexner. Pleasantville, N.Y.: Reader's Digest, 1975. 896 pp.

This is more extensive than its folksy title might suggest and it is reasonably up-to-date. It is basically a dictionary of undiscriminated synonyms, yet it includes a good deal of material that overlaps with dictionary entries, such as notes on usage, etymology, and pronunciation. For the user with a good dictionary, it is partly redundant.

Roget's II: The New Thesaurus. The editors of the *American Heritage Dictionary.* Boston: Houghton Mifflin, 1980. 1072 pp.

This is the newest and most publicized of current synonymies, but the final point made in connection with the *Family Word Finder* applies even more strongly to this title. Although it is authoritative and its format is as innovative as its publishers claim, its substance steers the thesaurus back towards the dictionary rather than into new territory. It establishes a new form between dictionaries of

undiscriminated and discriminated synonyms. Word definitions are given higher priority, along with the extensive usage labels which are so much the hallmark of *American Heritage* lexicography. Synonyms are painstakingly aligned with meanings so that you cannot make a mistake. If you feel unsure at the learning trade, you will appreciate this conservatism, but if you are more experienced, it is superfluous.

Sample Questions for Synonym Books

1. What word can I substitute for *habeas corpus?*

2. How many words can I find that refer to long periods of time?

3. What is an informal word for "prestidigitate"?

4. What range of concepts are generally opposed to the notion of free will?

5. I've used the word "relationship" too many times in this paper. What other word can I substitute?

6. I'm not finding any information in the subject catalogue under "tariff." What other term could I look under?

7. Is the word "egghead" associated just with intelligence or with a lot of education? What is a more formal synonym?

8. What are some of the ideas that are associated with the concept of "force"?

9. What expression can I use for "make your bed and lie in it" that isn't a cliché?

10. What word can I replace "skepticism" with that refers particularly to religious skepticism?

WES THE COLLEGE CAT

In pondering over the numerous images and symbols which recur throughout James Joyce's A Portrait of the Artist as a Young Man one can, no doubt, find a myriad of rather obvious topics

for an essay of the prescribed length and qualifications. Indeed, of manifest organizational themes this work has no shortage. To transcend the plainly obvious, however, and to expound on the less evident of those themes,

is our aim, even at the risk
(always present when dealing
with the less-than-obvious)
of confusing the
simple-minded.

THAT'S THE KIND OF
STUFF MY MOTHER
TAUGHT ME TO BURY
WHEN I WAS A
KITTEN.

3. WRITING GUIDES

Your damned nonsense can I stand twice or once, but sometimes always, my God, never.

Sviatoslav Richter (1914–   ) to the second flute at Covent Garden

Writing is an important part of learning—to many it is the most important part—so you need a tool to give you information about writing. Among the hundreds of writing guides on the market, not just any will fill this need. Most are designed to be used in composition courses; some are meant only to develop college-level writing "readiness"; others are workbooks, not texts. Style manuals (see Chapter 6) and even dictionaries contain information about writing, but not enough. For a variety of reasons, many of the titles you encounter while browsing in a bookstore or buying books for classes turn out not to be the ones you should have sitting on your desk when you embark alone on a typical writing task. Here are some thoughts about getting the right one.

SCOPE

The masses of writing guides can be divided into several types (excluding some technical handbooks and admitting misleading titles): readers; guides to writing about literature; rhetorics; grammars; and composition books. Of these, readers are not meant for reference and guides to writing about

literature are narrower than you need. Rhetorics give information mainly about the large-scale or strategic features of argument. Grammars, at the opposite extreme, deal on a small scale with meaning in sentence units. Composition books try to cover the material of both rhetorics and grammars, and add some material on research besides. The first four types are useful as texts for classes, while the last type is the best to own for general reference.

TONE

What you need for reference should be simply and sympathetically written but not written "down," because you will be using it at several different stages in your learning career.

LEVEL

A good reference book for writing should do a maximum of informing and a minimum of selling because you should be consulting it more for instruction than for motivation. If you still need to be cajoled into writing you are not ready for this tool. Composition books that devote most of their attention to so-called pre-writing, or to helping you get in touch with what you see, taste, smell, touch, hear, or recoil from are excellent for beginning writers but not general enough to be good reference tools.

Next, the book should cover material at several levels. Nobody wants to buy a new writing guide every few years. Certainly, it should present the material you first encounter in elementary or high school, such as definitions for the parts of speech and lists of transitional devices to unify or link paragraphs. But, as you get beyond that, you will also need to consult, say, grammatical information about more complicated sentence structures, a section on reasoning, a sample research paper, or illustrations of several different tones and styles. You may even want some information on controversial subjects, such as how to avoid sexist language. Finally, if you are using a writing guide at all, you are ready to profit from

some details about the choices involved in writing to replace
the rules-and-regulations attitude of primers.

ORDER

The book's parts should follow what might be called a re-
constructive order, one that reinforces your appreciation of
the basic steps in writing well, in particular reinforcing large-
scale matters over small-scale ones. For instance, it is helpful
to have the material on rhetoric come before the material on
grammar; and, within the material on rhetoric, as much con-
solidation as possible of the traditional modes is desirable.
Finally, all the book's sections should be independent. Since
you will only consult the book from time to time, you do not
want a book that is organized as a continuous, cumulative
narrative.

In addition, you want a book that takes a more or less
traditional approach in its organization. This criterion might
raise fears that the work would be stodgy, but this is not
necessarily the case. The goal is simply efficient reference. A
traditional composition book will use terms that are more familiar to you, examples that are clearer.

FORMAT

Extremely detailed indexing is essential for writing guides,
as is the case in all reference tools. Also, the text should be
heavily and clearly sectioned. The subject matter should be
divided into many small, discrete units. Numbers and letters
for sections, rules or shading, variations in type size, style and
color and spacing adjustments should all be used with a heavy
hand to direct you as quickly as possible to the material you
need. While these devices are, from one point of view, arbitrary and artificial, they are no more so than similar devices in
other sorts of reference books, and are certainly no less helpful.

A good reference book for writing should have examples for
every instruction it gives; it also should have exercises for as

many instructions as possible, preferably with answers. (Very few composition books give answer tables, but many have accompanying free instructors' manuals; you should try to obtain these.) While other conventional reference works do not have exercises, the opportunity a composition book offers to practice writing skills right along with gaining information about them is particularly advantageous.

TIMELINESS AND AUTHORITY

As to timeliness, language being what it is, the information in composition books changes slowly, although the examples may be more or less appealing depending on their contemporaneity. Choose the latest edition of a particular title, and choose a book written in the '80s over one written in the '60s, but do not treat a difference of less than ten years as determinative.

As to authority, it is a volatile criterion when you are judging composition books. In general, books that have gone through three or more editions pass the test of authority, but no one would argue that authoritativeness increases with number of editions. The reputations of the publisher and of the author also count.

Once you have applied all of these criteria, you should be glad to find a relatively small number of books meeting them all. Below is a comparison of about a dozen of the texts most popularly assigned in composition classes or recommended by various reference sources and thus most likely to be considered as reference books for writing. In each group, the listing follows an order of preference.

Recommended

Gorrell, Robert M., and Charlton Laird. *Modern English Handbook*. Englewood Cliffs, N.J.: Prentice-Hall, 1976. 494 pp.

Crews, Frederick. *The Random House Handbook*. 3rd ed. New York: Random House, 1980. 435 pp.

Photograph by D. C. Bell.

McCrimmon, James M. *Writing with a Purpose*. 7th ed.
    Boston: Houghton Mifflin, 1980. 557 pp.
Irmscher, William F. *The Holt Guide to English*. 3rd ed. New
    York: Holt, Rinehart & Winston, 1981. 554 pp.

These books are similar in most basic respects. They cover
the widest scope of material in this type of reference book.
They are written for a general audience, covering from basic
to quite sophisticated levels of material. They are designed to
serve both as reference and as teaching texts—they provide
comparatively detailed explanations of the material and they
try to make the information interesting and convincing as well
as understandable. They are sensibly designed and ordered,
with units of material well-separated and given proper priority. They provide many examples associated with the material, frequently from student writing and often of the before-
and-after sort to help you appreciate writing as a process.
Each has numerous exercises. Although none of them has an
answer key, all have instructors' manuals.

Good (Handbooks)

Fowler, H. Ramsey. *The Little, Brown Handbook*. Boston: Lit-
    tle, Brown, 1980. 554 pp.
Leggett, Glenn, C. David Mead, and William Charvat, eds.
    Prentice-Hall Handbook for Writers. 8th ed. Englewood
    Cliffs, N.J.: Prentice-Hall, 1982. 544 pp.
Shaw, Harry. *The Harper Handbook of College Composition*. 5th
    ed. New York: Harper & Row, 1981. 609 pp.
Elsbree, Langdon, Frederick Bracher, and Nell Altizer, eds.
    Heath's College Handbook of Composition. 10th ed. Lex-
    ington, Mass.: D.C. Heath, 1981. 448 pp.
Hodges, John C., and Mary E. Whitten, eds. *Harbrace College
    Handbook*. 9th ed. New York: Harcourt Brace Jovano-
    vich, 1982. 586 pp.
Millward, Celia. *Handbook for Writers*. New York: Holt,
    Rinehart & Winston, 1980. 494 pp.
Guth, Hans P. *New English Handbook*. Belmont, Calif.: Wads-
    worth, 1982. 494 pp.

Photograph by D. C. Bell.

Kierzek, John M., and Walker Gibson, eds. Rev. by Robert
   F. Willson, Jr. *The Macmillan Handbook of English.* 6th ed.
   New York: Macmillan, 1977. 520 pp.
Ebbitt, David, and Wilma R. Ebbitt, eds. *Writer's Guide and
   Index to English.* 7th ed. Glenview, Ill.: Scott, Foresman,
   1982. 702 pp.

The main difference between the first eight of these and the
recommended books is that these are less concerned with explanation and justification. In other words, they have a less
problem-oriented approach. They are more prescriptive. The
term handbook is genuinely suited to them: they are more
compact books overall and their size is smaller. They tend to
have less material on rhetoric and style and more on grammar
and research mechanics of various sorts, perhaps because the
latter subjects lend themselves to prescription. In level, they
are less comprehensive than the recommended group, con-
centrating more on basics. Their order tends to follow the
emphasis in scope just noted; that is, the sections on large-
scale rhetorical matters often come later rather than earlier.
All of them have relatively few examples in which they dem-
onstrate several progressive steps for dealing with a writing
task, as opposed to presenting samples of good and bad. They
generally have simple, short exercises. Differences among
them do exist and are reflected in the order of preference, but
these are not always obvious.
   Writer's Guide and Index is unusual for this group because it
comes in two parts. (They have been issued both together and
separately.) While the *Guide*'s sections on certain rhetorical
subjects rival that in the recommended books above, the *Index*
makes it more like a handbook. This work is less convenient to
use than the books in any category here because you must
switch back and forth between *Guide* and *Index*.

Fair

Barnet, Sylvan, and Marcia Stubbs. *Barnet & Stubbs's Practical
   Guide to Writing.* 3rd ed. Boston: Little, Brown, 1980.
   424 pp.

Hall, Donald and Clayton Hudnall. *Writing Well*. 4th ed.
     Boston: Little, Brown, 1982. 432 pp.
Baker, Sheridan. *The Complete Stylist and Handbook*. 2nd ed.
     New York: Harper & Row, 1980. 494 pp.
McMahan, Elizabeth, and Susan Day. *The Writer's Rhetoric and
     Handbook*. New York: McGraw-Hill, 1980. 450 pp.

The first two books in this group are fine teaching texts but
not efficient reference tools. The second two are hybrids between the recommended books and the handbooks, but provide less than either.

Not Recommended

Baker, Sheridan. *The Practical Stylist*. 5th ed. New York:
     Harper & Row, 1980. 224 pp.
Strunk, William Jr., and E. B. White. *The Elements of Style*.
     3rd ed. New York: Macmillan, 1979. 85 pp.
Zinsser, William. *On Writing Well*. New York: Harper &
     Row, 1976. 151 pp.

The Elements of Style is one of America's best-selling writing
guides and the other two in this group are also much assigned,
but none of them is as comprehensive as the books in the
groups above. As the emphasis is on style in at least two of the
titles shows, they are not designed with breadth in mind. All
three are lively to read, but their use for reference has the
narrowest of limits.

No honest review of reference books for writing could end
without acknowledging the large number of writing teachers
who deny the efficacy of any such tool. They say books like
the ones listed above are as helpless to promote good writing
as *The Joy of Sex* is to promote good sex. No doubt. Do not
expect keys to the kingdom. Be aware of the difference between information and skill. Simply start with information.

Sample Questions for Writing Guides

1. Do all papers have to have introductions?

2. What is the difference between plagiarizing and paraphrasing?

3. I know one-sentence paragraphs are incorrect, but is there an upper limit for paragraph length too?

4. How long does the conclusion of a short paper have to be?

5. How can I write so as to sound authoritative?

6. A paper of mine was returned with the comment "parallelism" written next to several sentences. What does that mean?

7. I'm required to hand in an outline with my next paper, but I've forgotten the exact requirements of outline form. Where can I find them?

8. What did my English professor mean by the comment that I need to pay attention to my writing style? I didn't make any grammatical mistakes.

9. How can I change the subordination in this passage to convey my thoughts more clearly?

10. My paper is too short (long). How can I expand (shorten) it?

Thoughts on Writing Guides

4. ONE-VOLUME GENERAL ENCYCLOPEDIAS

To grow mature with pure fact.

Charles Williams (1886–1945)

Some educators will tell you that the older you get, the less you need a one-volume general encyclopedia. That depends. The tool can be extremely helpful if you get a good one and approach it with the right spirit. You will soon find out how to identify a good one; for now, turn your attention to the right spirit.

If you are like most people, you have probably gone through two stages in your attitude toward general encyclopedias. In elementary school or junior high, you thought of encyclopedias as infallible and universal sources of knowledge. The word "encyclopedia" itself is rooted in the notion of a comprehensive circle, or complete system of learning. Later on in your schooling, however, you probably turned against these ideal mentors, criticizing them as dated, parochial, and shallow. Teachers usually have their own reasons for reinforcing these attitudes at both stages: they want younger students to respect book knowledge, but they want older ones to probe beyond the least challenging sources of information. Often, the stage of disdain lasts a lifetime.

The fashions today in one-volume encyclopedias run toward the interdisciplinary or illustrative. On one hand, you can find encyclopedias such as *Notable American Women* and *The Harvard Encyclopedia of American Ethnic Groups;* on the other, ones such as

Comparisons and *What's What*. Perhaps these are the necessary
consequences of dislike for general encyclopedias. Or maybe
they indicate suspicion that a computer console will soon replace the encyclopedia, anyway. Before you give up on general
knowledge altogether, however, or until you can afford that
computer console, there are three main ways in which a general
encyclopedia can help you learn. (1) It can prompt you on facts
you remember only vaguely, such as names, dates, and labels
that seem to be on the tip of your mind. The brief and highly
specific information that a good dictionary provides does not
always fill in such memory gaps. (2) It can serve as a foil in your
thinking, the way one debater serves as a foil for the other, or an
hypothesis serves as a foil in a scientific experiment. As an
established body of information and opinion, it is ready-made
for you to oppose, correct, support, refine, or expand. (3) It can
introduce you to an unfamiliar subject. If you are a liberal arts
student, you will especially need this aid since you are expected
to gain knowledge that is broad, but even if you are a computer
science trainee you might want to look up "Electoral College"
in a presidential election year, "Islam" during a Middle Eastern
clash, or "Measles" when vaccination notices come out from
school. If you look for these three benefits from a general
encyclopedia you will not be putting the encyclopedia on a
pedestal, but neither will you be going to the other extreme and
discrediting the tool. In all three cases you will be an active
participant in the learning process.

Because a general encyclopedia in one volume is closer to the
scale of the average mind than one in many volumes, it can
probably serve you better. Besides, when your mind needs a
prompter, or a foil, or a guide, you are often off someplace
where no multivolume encyclopedia is likely to be.

Now let's see how these points about the right spirit apply to
choosing a good one-volume general encyclopedia.

AUTHORITY, ACCURACY,
TIMELINESS

Authority, accuracy and timeliness are the first testing
points for all encyclopedias. Each must prove its worth by

listing its editors and contributors so that you can check these persons' qualifications. Accuracy you can assess by checking subjects that you already know something about. Timeliness is a bit harder to judge, considering that every ad says "new" and copyright dates do not always discriminate between thorough or cursory revisions. Find out from the preface or the articles exactly how recent an encyclopedia's information is. No encyclopedia is ever up-to-the-minute, but you should try to find one current within ten years. When evaluating an encyclopedia for timeliness, besides checking articles where a recent date is obviously important (i.e. "Nuclear Energy") check at least one article where knowledge does not shift so fast—say, "John Milton"—because that sort of article is the most likely to be slighted by the encyclopedia's revisers.

COVERAGE

Look for coverage of as many different kinds of people, places, things and ideas as possible. Full depth of coverage is neither possible nor desirable. That is for specialized encyclopedias and texts. At the least, however, a one-volume general encyclopedia should give more explanation than a dictionary. Also, it should have bibliographies.

Coverage in terms of fairness where facts are at issue is a criterion on which almost all encyclopedia authorities concur. It is a hard criterion to apply, though. Since factuality is a matter of degree, an ideal fairness is impossible to come by in an encyclopedia of any sort, and perhaps should not even be attempted. One compromise would be for an article simply to acknowledge the existence of information other than what it provides; another would be for an article to provide enough depth so that fairness can be achieved indirectly. For instance, fairness about the subject of evolution does not necessarily mean saying that creationists dispute Darwin's theory of natural selection; instead, it may mean explaining the theory of natural selection fully enough for its various limitations and problems to become evident. Overall, be more concerned about the number and diversity of subjects a one-volume general encyclopedia covers, and about the balance it strikes between

minor and major subjects, than about the range of opinions it presents on a single subject.

READABILITY

Since a one-volume general encyclopedia is consulted most often on unfamiliar subjects, articles that use a specialized vocabulary about subjects such as "Isomers," "Impressionism," or "Ibsen" will not help you much. Difficulties with readability actually come up most often in multivolume or specialized encyclopedias, however. In one-volume general ones, the editors try so hard to reach a wide market that they more often aim at an audience that is less than college-educated.

FORMAT

Since you are going to consult your encyclopedia often, you want convenience. Look for a comfortable typeface and type size, and a format that provides plenty of space. Illustrations are generally helpful, sometimes absolutely necessary, and always engaging, although once in a while they can be confusing if poorly captioned or placed. Tables, graphs, and other arrangements of material different from the prose paragraph are as helpful as illustrations, with the same caveats. These remarks all have to do with the convenience of the format in a visual sense. Another need the user has, however, is for convenience in a bibliographical sense. The names for subjects should be easy to find and getting to information should not require more than one step.

There are two basic arrangements for encyclopedias. One offers short articles on limited topics. This is the "specific entry" or the "alphabetical" arrangement. It necessitates many cross-references and sometimes special indexes or guides to point out the complicated contexts into which its small pieces can fit. The other arrangement offers longer articles that do the synthesizing for you. This is the "broad entry" or the "topical" arrangement. Its problem is that the particular synthesis it

offers may not be exactly the one you need and so, again, a special index is necessary.

Differences in arrangement have effects other than practical ones. For instance, the alphabetical arrangement seems suited to the twentieth-century specialization of knowledge, while the topical suits the hope for unity. A related issue is whether you or the encyclopedia should be in charge. The alphabetical arrangement puts you more in charge in the sense that you are the one who must arrange the parts of knowledge into a whole. The encyclopedia is only the beginning. Interpreted crudely, the topical arrangement is the opposite—it presumes to offer you knowledge already whole. The encyclopedia is the end. During the time encyclopedias have been written, both arrangements have had their champions and their challengers, and recently, encyclopedists have tried to combine both.

Recommended

Harris, William H., and Judith S. Levey, eds. *New Columbia Encyclopedia.* 4th ed. New York: Columbia University Press, 1975. 3052 pp.

General consensus finds *New Columbia* best among one-volume general encyclopedias. Such consensus is rare, but justified.

New Columbia can be given high marks on accuracy. This is not surprising, since it prides itself on being the most authoritative of the one-volume general encyclopedias, supporting that reputation by its association with Columbia University, many of whose faculty have contributed articles. (No articles are signed, however.)

As to timeliness, *New Columbia* keeps its material up-to-date reasonably well, with information current through 1974.

In breadth of coverage, *New Columbia* contains more material than any other one-volume general encyclopedia, about twice as much as its largest competitors. Although using quantitative measures

controlled fusion is achieved, it will have great advantages over fission as a source of energy. Deuterium is relatively easy to obtain, since it constitutes a small percentage of the hydrogen in water and can be separated by electrolysis, in contrast to the complex and expensive methods required to extract uranium-235 from its sources. Yet the most pressing problem of nuclear energy is not the technological difficulties that must be overcome to provide large quantities of this energy for peaceful uses but the threat to the continued existence of the human race posed by the vast stockpiles of nuclear weapons held by the major national governments (see DISARMAMENT, NUCLEAR). See Irene D. Jaworski and Alexander Joseph, *Atomic Energy* (1961); C. N. Martin, *The Atom: Friend or Foe* (1962); Samuel Glasstone, *Sourcebook on Atomic Energy* (3d ed. 1967); Harry Foreman, ed., *Nuclear Power and the Public* (1970); Irving Adler, *Atomic Energy* (1971); Richard C. Lewis, *Nuclear Power Rebellion: Citizen vs. the Atomic Industrial Establishment* (1972).

nuclear magnetic resonance: see MAGNETIC RESONANCE.

nuclear physics, study of the components, structure, and behavior of the NUCLEUS of the atom. It is especially concerned with the nature of matter and with NUCLEAR ENERGY. The subject is commonly divided into three fields: low-energy nuclear physics, the study of RADIOACTIVITY; medium-energy nuclear physics, the study of the force between nuclear particles; and high-energy nuclear physics, the study of the transformations among subatomic particles in reactions produced in a PARTICLE ACCELERATOR. See ELEMENTARY PARTICLES.

nuclear reactor, device for producing controlled release of NUCLEAR ENERGY. A fission reactor consists basically of a mass of fissionable material usually types, in which discrete fuel elements are surrounded by a moderator, are called heterogeneous reactors. If the fissionable fuel elements are intimately mixed with a moderator, the system is called a homogeneous reactor (e.g., a reactor having a core of a liquid uranium compound dissolved in heavy water). The breeder reactor is a special type used to produce more fissionable atoms than it consumes. It must first be primed with certain isotopes of uranium or plutonium that release more neutrons than are needed to continue the chain reaction at a constant rate. In an ordinary reactor, any surplus neutrons are absorbed in nonfissionable control rods made of a substance, such as boron or cadmium, that readily absorbs neutrons. In a breeder reactor, however, these surplus neutrons are used to transmute certain nonfissionable atoms into fissionable atoms. Thorium (Th-232) can be converted by neutron bombardment into fissionable U-233. Similarly, U-238, the most common isotope of uranium, can be converted by neutron bombardment into fissionable plutonium-239. These transmutations have made possible the large-scale production of atomic energy. The excess nuclear fuel produced can be extracted and used in other reactors or in nuclear weapons. The heat energy released by fission in a reactor heats a liquid or gas coolant that circulates in and out of the reactor core, usually becoming radioactive. Outside the core, the coolant circulates through a heat exchanger where the heat is transferred to another medium. This second medium, nonradioactive since it has not circulated in the reactor core, carries the heat away from the reactor. This heat energy can be dissipated or it can be used to drive conventional heat engines that generate usable power. Atomic power stations are now in service in various parts of the world, including the United States, the USSR, and Great Britain. Submarines and surface ships propelled by nuclear reactors are in operation, and adaptation of nuclear reactors for use in rockets, aircraft, and locomotives is in progress. The design of nuclear fusion reactors, which are still in the experimental stage, differs considerably from that of fission reactors. In a fusion reactor, the principal problem is the containment of the PLASMA fuel, which must be at a temperature of millions of degrees in order to initiate the reaction.

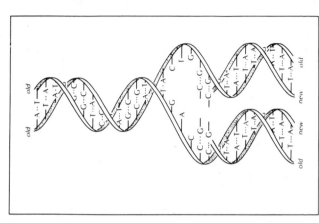

were coiled into a double helix. In this model each nucleotide subunit along one strand is connected to a nucleotide subunit on the other strand by hydro-

Replication of strands of DNA

gen bonds between the base portions of the nucleotides. The fact that adenine only bonds with thymine (A—T) and guanine only bonds with cytosine (G—C) determines that the strands will be comple-

Power reactor system

pressure vessel   shielding   coolant passage

encased in shielding and provided with devices to regulate the rate of fission and an exchange system to extract the heat energy produced. Reactors can be used for research or for power production. A research reactor is designed to produce various beams of radiation for experimental application; the heat produced is a waste product and is dissipated as efficiently as possible. In a power reactor the heat produced is of primary importance for use in driving conventional heat engines; the beams of radiation are controlled by shielding. A reactor is so constructed that fission of atomic nuclei produces a self-sustaining nuclear CHAIN REACTION, in which the neutrons produced are able to split other nuclei. A chain reaction can be produced in a reactor by using uranium or plutonium in which the concentration of fissionable isotopes has been artificially increased. Even though the neutrons move at high velocities, the enriched fissionable isotope captures enough neutrons to make possible a self-sustaining chain reaction. In this type of reactor the neutrons carrying on the chain reaction are fast neutrons. A chain reaction can also be accomplished with a moderator to retard the neutrons so that they may be more easily captured by the fissionable atoms. The neutrons carrying on the chain reaction in this type of reactor are slow (or thermal) neutrons. Substances that can be used as moderators include graphite, beryllium, and heavy water (DEUTERIUM oxide). The moderator surrounds or is mixed with the fissionable fuel elements in the core of the reactor. A nuclear reactor is sometimes called an atomic pile because a reactor using graphite as a moderator consists of a pile of graphite blocks with rods of uranium fuel inserted into it. Reactors in which the uranium fuel are immersed in a bath of heavy water are often referred to as "swimming-pool" reactors. Reactors of these

Handbook, ed. by C. R. Tipton, Jr., et al. (4 vol., 2d ed. 1960–64); G. I. Bell, *Nuclear Reactor Theory* (1970).

nuclear structure: see NUCLEUS.

nuclear test-ban treaty: see DISARMAMENT, NUCLEAR.

nucleic acid, any of a group of organic substances, found in the chromosomes of living cells and viruses, that play an important role in the storage and replication of hereditary information and in protein synthesis. In most organisms, nucleic acids occur in combination with proteins; the combined substances are called nucleoproteins. Nucleic acid molecules are complex chains of varying length. The two chief types of nucleic acids are DNA (deoxyribonucleic acid), found mainly in the nuclei of normal cells, and RNA (ribonucleic acid), found mostly in the cytoplasm but also in small amounts in the nuclei, nucleoli, and chromosomes. A substance that he called nuclein (now known as DNA) was isolated in 1869 by Friedrich Miescher, but it was only recently that research revealed its significance as the material of which the GENE is composed, and thus its function as the chemical bearer of hereditary characteristics. The amount of RNA varies from cell to cell, but the amount of DNA is constant for all typical cells of any given species of plant or animal, no matter what the size or function of that cell. This amount doubles as the chromosomes replicate themselves before cell division takes place (see MITOSIS); in the ovum and sperm the amount is half that in the body cells (see MEIOSIS). The chemical and physical properties of DNA suit it for both replication and transfer of information. Each DNA molecule is a long two-stranded chain. The chains are made up of subunits called nucleotides, each containing a sugar (deoxyribose), a phosphate group, and one of four nitrogenous bases, adenine, guanine, thymine, and cytosine, denoted A, G, T, and C respectively. The information carried by genes is coded in sequences of nucleotides, which correspond to sequences of amino acids in the polypeptide chains of proteins. In 1953 the molecular biologists J. D. Watson, an American, and F. H. Crick, an Englishman, proposed that the two DNA strands

sure that DNA can be replicated, i.e., that identical copies can be made in order to be transmitted to the next generation. In order to be expressed as protein, the genetic information must be carried to the protein-synthesizing machinery of the cell, which is usually in the cell's cytoplasm (see CELL). One form of RNA mediates this process. RNA is similar to DNA, but contains the sugar ribose instead of deoxyribose, and the base uracil (U) instead of thymine. To initiate the process of information transfer, one strand of the double-stranded DNA chain serves as a template for the synthesis of a single strand of RNA that is complementary to the DNA strand. This process is called transcription, and—like all steps in protein synthesis—it is mediated by enzymes. The newly synthesized RNA, called messenger RNA, or mRNA, moves quickly to bodies in the cytoplasm called ribosomes. Each ribosome is the site of synthesis of a polypeptide chain. Clusters of ribosomes, called polyribosomes, or polysomes, attach to the mRNA so that many polypeptide chains are synthesized from the same mRNA. Ribosomes are composed of noninformational ribonucleic acid bound to a protein. The nucleotide sequence of the mRNA is translated into the amino acid sequence of a protein by adaptor molecules composed of a third type of RNA called transfer RNA, or tRNA. There are at least 20 different species of tRNA, with each species binding one of the 20 amino acids. In protein synthesis, a nucleotide sequence along the mRNA does not specify an amino acid directly; rather, it specifies a particular species of tRNA. For example, in coding for the amino acid tyrosine, a nucleotide sequence of mRNA is complementary to a portion of a tyrosine-tRNA molecule. As each specified tRNA associates with its complementary space on the mRNA, the tRNA releases its amino acid, which is added onto the lengthening protein chain. When the protein chain is complete, it is released from the ribosome site. The particular sequence of amino acids in each polypeptide chain is determined by the genetic code. Starting at one end of the mRNA strand, each 3-nucleotide sequence, or codon, specifies one amino acid, and a series of such codons specifies a polypeptide chain. Although a "vocabulary" of 64 words, or specifications, is theoreti-

can be notoriously risky for encyclopedias, as for dictionaries, in this case the numbers seem to substantiate *New Columbia*'s reputation as the most comprehensive encyclopedia in its class. Certainly it spreads widest in its biographical and geographical articles. Its editors say it has particularly expanded its coverage of Africa, Asia and South America.

In depth of coverage, *New Columbia* also excels. Its articles manage to make their subjects coherent. For instance, under "John Milton," *New Columbia* conveys the complications of the English poet's life while preserving the sense of constancy in his aims and the singularity of his achievement. Other encyclopedias' entries, which give Milton's birth and death dates, a few other pieces of information about his career, and the titles of some of his works, are not only shorter, but, regrettably, more fragmented. *New Columbia* treats subjects in science and technology deeply in the sense of providing detail, but says little about the social impact of particular advances in scientific knowledge, despite the fact that these are of most interest to people who are not scientists (see "Nuclear Energy" and "TV"). Nor does it usually explain scientific subjects by organizing the information chronologically, despite the fact that such a perspective almost always aids nonspecialists' understanding (see "Motion"). An impressive feature of *New Columbia* is that it provides bibliographies— not for all subjects, unfortunately, but for the most important ones. Conveniently placed at the end of each article, they always help, often represent a fine review, and sometimes even make up for what a particular article may lack in coverage. *New Columbia* does well with objectivity. To take a random example: on the subject of Chilean Salvadore Allende's death, *New Columbia* says that published reports were of suicide, while Allende's wife called it murder. Other encyclopedias say merely that Allende "died."

New Columbia has not radically simplified its vo-

cabulary, and may present some difficulties even to scholars, particularly in entries on science and technology. The sophisticated vocabulary in *New Columbia* is not prohibitive. Rather, it assures that you will not outgrow this encyclopedia.

The specific entry arrangement is used for *New Columbia*, but enough attention has been paid to the cross-references so that it is easy to use.

New Columbia's layout is not particularly attractive. It does employ a modern, streamlined typeface in a relatively large size, so that users do not have to strain when they read. Extra space is minimal, however, and this encyclopedia has very few illustrations compared with its competitors. Some black-and-white drawings and diagrams accompany mainly scientific entries, and black and white maps are provided on useful scales. Also, quite a bit of information is tabularized, as in other encyclopedias, and comes across clearly. Overall, although the editors have cared for the reader's eye regarding the print and a few other aspects of organizing information, they have not emphasized graphics.

New Columbia weighs slightly over 10 pounds. When you pull it off your shelf you have to use caution. If you want to use an encyclopedia that is more portable, *The Concise Columbia Encyclopedia* (1983) may seem to be a good substitute. Its editorship makes it authoritative, and of course it is more timely than its parent, but with less than one-third of the entries, one-sixth the number of words, and no bibliographies, it cannot be recommended over *New Columbia*.

Good

Mitchell, James, ed. in chief. *The Random House Encyclopedia.* New York: Random House, 1977. 2856 pp.

Random House is *New Columbia's* chief competitor.

It is on the same scale in terms of its size and goals. Its
major differences from *New Columbia* lie in its emphasis on illustrations and its separation into two
parts—really two different volumes—called the Colorpedia and the Alphapedia, the first of which em-
ploys broad entry arrangement; the second, specific
entry. Within this broad comparison/contrast, other
similarities and differences emerge.

Random House has a fine reputation for accuracy,
although in strictly quantitative terms it does not
include as many facts and figures as *New Columbia*. It
does treat some subjects that are more current than
ones in *New Columbia* (you can find out who Mark
Spitz is only from *Random House*) or includes more
current information in its articles on other subjects,
because of its slightly later publication date.

Coverage differs significantly between the two
rivals. *Random House* has biographical and geographical entries that are less broad than those in *New
Columbia*, and, with a few exceptions, it does not
have anywhere near *New Columbia's* depth. The rationale for short entries in the Alphapedia is that the
Colorpedia will provide fuller explanations. The 893
topics covered in the Colorpedia have all been treated at 1400 words, however, a length that is not
equally appropriate for all subjects.

Random House does provide bibliographies but
these are hard to find and are much less satisfactory,
for varied reasons, than those in *New Columbia*.

Two advantages of *Random House's* coverage are
that it seems to treat more subjects in the area of
psychology than *New Columbia*, and on scientific
subjects, it does not have *New Columbia's* previously
mentioned shortcomings.

Random House has a more simplified vocabulary
than *New Columbia*—it is advertised as a family encyclopedia—and the level of its explanations is excellent for introductory purposes. On many subjects
you will find it too elementary, but on others you
will be surprised at its clarity.

Random House combines both systems of entry arrangement, as has been noted, but emphasizes the Colorpedia, the part that is topically arranged. You look up a subject in the Alphapedia and, if you want to go further, flip to one or more entries in the Colorpedia. This two- three- or four-step process can be not only time-consuming but confusing, as when the Alphapedia and Colorpedia entries conflict with each other (see the two entries on thermodynamics, for example), or when the Alphapedia entry is wrong (see "Francis Bacon"). Furthermore, information in the Colorpedia is scattered, some of it appearing in the text and some of it in the captions for illustrations. The bibliographies suffer from fragmentation too. They come in an appendix, rather than in the encyclopedia's main text, and are grouped according to the Colorpedia's topical headings, so that readings on particular short subjects are hard to find. In general, all this fragmentation hardly seems worth the synthesis the Colorpedia provides, especially given the questionable merits of synthesis in the first place.

Random House's illustrations are impressive. They not only make the encyclopedia easy to read but they add depth, in many cases, to the entries. The photographs of people in the Alphapedia are especially attractive to see. A particularly good secondary effect of the illustrations is to make the whole encyclopedia seem more practical and action-oriented. For instance, pictures showing several steps in the physical production of encyclopedias take the topic "Reference Books" out of the ivory tower. The illustrations are not always helpful, however. Sometimes their meaning is not sufficiently explained in a caption; sometimes they are unnecessarily complicated. In such cases they seem to become ends in themselves.

Random House does include a great deal of information and opinion, its illustrations are impressive, and it is highly readable, but it is difficult to use and that

process will spread explosively through the fissionable material.

In order to generate electricity the process must be slowed down and controlled, and means must be provided for removing the heat. There is a higher probability of the fission occurring in U-235 if the neutron absorbed is moving relatively slowly, about 1.2mi (2km) per second. For this reason special materials such as graphite or deuterium, called moderators, are incorporated into the atomic pile in order to slow down the neutrons.

The amount of fissionable material brought together is crucial for a sustained chain reaction. If more neutrons are lost by absorption or escape than are produced, the reaction will not be self-sustaining. If more neutrons are produced than are lost on average, a self-sustaining and expanding reaction occurs. The smallest amount in which fission is self-sustaining is called the critical mass. In an atomic pile it is necessary to keep the flux of neutrons nearly in balance and constant. To control the reaction rate in a pile, rods of neutron-absorb-

ing material can be moved in and out as required [8].

Fast reactors and their make-up

Structural supports in atomic piles are made of materials that absorb as few neutrons as possible. Fast reactors have a small core of fissile material and no moderator to slow the neutrons. There is little absorbent material and few neutrons are wasted. Natural uranium is 99.3 percent U-238 and 0.7 percent U-235. While U-235 is fissionable, U-238 is not, but after absorbing a neutron can decay radioactively to plutonium Pu-239, which is. Atomic bombs and fast reactors require fairly pure fissionable material, so U-235 must be separated out—for example in a giant diffusion plant—or U-238 turned into Pu-239 in a reactor and separated chemically. In a fast reactor, the fissile core is surrounded by a blanket of natural uranium so that neutrons escaping from the core can turn U-238 into Pu-239. If more fissionable material is made than consumed the reactor, or pile, is called a breeder reactor.

KEY

The mushroom cloud of an atomic explosion haunts civilization. Although the spread of nuclear weapons has been banned by treaties, and some nations have accepted technical limitations on testing, the number of countries with access to nuclear weaponry continues to grow.

5 The nucleus of an atom, containing protons (red) and neutrons (brown), may change to produce radioactivity. gamma rays (electromagnetic radiation, violet), beta rays (electrons or positrons, grey), and alpha particles (helium ions, orange). Naturally radioactive uranium-238 [A] decays as shown to form lead. [B] shows the decay of cobalt.

U-235
U-236
Te-135
Xe-135

5

A U-238 92 146
Th-234 90 144
Pa-234 91 143

B Co-60 27 33
Ni-60 28 32

C Sr-90 38 52
Y-90 39 51

6

more uranium-235 [3] and lead to a chain reaction, or be absorbed by other atoms [4] or U-238 [5].

7 The mass spectrograph of Francis Aston (1877–1945) showed that elements are formed of separate isotopes, each nearly an integral multiple of the mass of a proton. Later spectrometers gave exact measurements of the masses of nuclei and are used to distinguish isotopes

8 Nuclear reactors are the power houses of the future and to some extent of the present. But the formidable problems they create in disposal of radioactive wastes have not yet been satisfactorily solved. Automatic checking of the rate of the chain reaction within an atomic pile is needed so that control rods can be inserted to regulate the reaction rate

Reproduced with permission from *The Random House Encyclopedia*. Copyright © 1977 by Mitchell-Beazley, London, England; distributed in the U.S. by Random House. "Mushroom cloud" photograph courtesy Photri.

difficulty is not compensated by superior breadth or depth of coverage.

Other

Shapiro, Max S., and William Jaber, eds. *The Cadillac Modern Encyclopedia*. St. Louis, Mo.: Cadillac Publishing Co., 1973.

> Not as timely as others besides being more limited in length and breadth. Out of print for several years with no plan for revision.

Horsley, E. M., ed. *The New Hutchinson Twentieth Century Encyclopedia*. Great Britain: Hutchinson Publishing Group, 1978.

> Emphasis on Great Britain.

Seibert, William, ed. *The New Lincoln Library Encyclopedia*. 3 vols. Columbus, Ohio: Frontier Press, 1979.

> Formerly one volume, but has expanded. Topical arrangement only.

Friedhoff, Herman, and Ben Lenthall, eds. *The University Desk Encyclopedia*. New York: E. P. Dutton, 1977.

> Out of print for several years with no plan for revision.

Sample Questions for One-Volume General Encyclopedias

1. What is Plato's "Myth of the Cave," why do professors think it's so important, and where can I read it?

2. Who were the Druids and what did they believe?

3. I know that Washington, D.C. was named for George Washington, but did he have anything to do with selecting and planning the city as the capitol of the U.S.?

4. Would it be appropriate to call the Colorado River one of the most important rivers in the world?

5. I've heard the word "entropy" used a lot, but I can't understand the definition in the dictionary. It seems to be a word from physics, but if I look it up in a physics dictionary I'm sure I won't understand the definition there either. What does "entropy" mean, and how come it's used so widely?

6. What are the rules for writing a sonnet?

7. What is the difference between "average," "median," and "mean?"

8. What African country did Idi Amin head?

9. Has a woman ever won the Nobel Prize?

10. Is Ernest Hemingway considered one of the world's great writers, or is he only important to Americans?

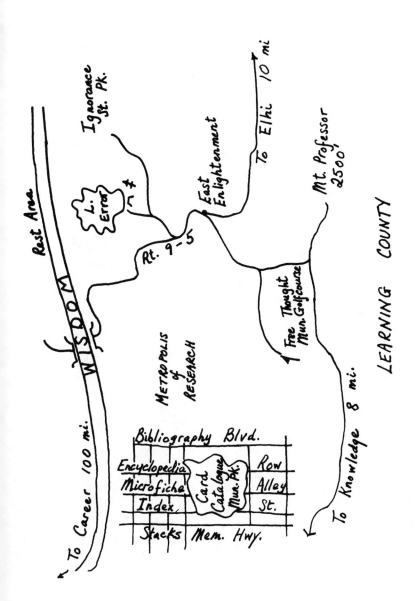

5. RESEARCH GUIDES

. . . the knowledge of how to collect and use information is supplanting the machinery of the industrial age as the most effective technology for getting work accomplished.

"Careers in the 80's [sec. 12]," *The New York Times*, 14 October 1979, p. 15.

A research guide is a learner's map. It shows you the terrain of knowledge in a given academic field and aids you in choosing the best route to take while acquiring or extending that knowledge. Considering the helpfulness of these maps, it is surprising that they are so little used. They are seldom missing from their places on the reference shelves, ripped up, or ripped off. You may not even have heard of them, since many faculty never mention them.

Is a research guide necessary? Let's say you want to know if there are any specialized encyclopedias on religion and how accurate they are. Or your biology professor may have mentioned the importance of review articles to scientists and you are curious about what those are and where to find them. You wonder what a Marxist would say about *The Great Gatsby*, or how much you should care about what a Marxist would say. You think you might become a petroleum geologist, but need to know more about other subfields of geology before you decide. You want to find out where you can see more works by a modern painter you admire. You wish you could figure out how the "Government Documents" section of your library is organized. You need the names and addresses of the chairpeople of the three best graduate schools in music. You

are assigned to read five reviews of a book sparking recent controversy among economists and to assess the reviewers' biases. You must prepare for a meeting with your advisor to plan the research for your undergraduate thesis on alternative communities. A research guide will answer some of these questions directly; with others, it will help you by telling you where to turn. It can be put to good use for both beginning and advanced research problems. Consulting a research guide is a bit like consulting your own personal reference librarian. Although it cannot teach you all about a subject and is not the problem-solver to end all problems, it is getting to be more and more necessary. Information is coming at you like a tidal wave at exactly the same time as the methods for surviving tidal waves have changed and the money has been cut for classes in how to swim. Learners have always needed help in finding their way around the research materials for academic fields, but never more than now.

Research guides are extremely varied. Not all of them have even been considered for listing here; a great many have been ruled out because they are too long, or restricted, or out-dated, or uninstructive. The ones included may loosely be termed either descriptive or critical.

The descriptive guide is closest to a bibliography. It looks like a reference book, with heavily sectioned, short entries. It is classified and often annotated (that is why it is considered more than a bibliography) but the annotations do not make a point of comparison and recommendation. Assuming advanced users, it either ignores problems about the depth of learning it serves or assumes no such problems will arise. Most works with the words "guide to the literature" in their titles are descriptive.

The critical guide, on the other hand, usually looks like a text. It tries to deepen the learning it serves by explaining briefly about the field's actual content and method (as opposed to its tools), and by evaluating the tools themselves. It always covers elementary material but in the best cases it can be valuable to sophisticated researchers.

One other sort of guide must be mentioned, although it usually does not have the word "guide" in its title and only a couple of examples are listed below. This is the training guide,

or guide to the method of a field, as opposed to its literature, a guide that tells you how to test a hypothesis about *drosophila* genes or establish the original text of a play. Training guides overlap in some ways with critical guides. They are usually much more limited in their coverage of sources, however, and are never as systematic.

No matter what their type, all the guides have two general and related failings. They lag behind the development of new or newly important fields in their disciplines, and they do not adequately cover computerized research techniques. Guides in the humanities and social sciences are worse than those in the sciences, but even the latter have problems. Of course, these failings are largely unavoidable and do not destroy the guides' usefulness.

Among the three types, the critical research guide is the one that encompasses the most, and can be considered a basic learning tool. Because few ideal critical guides exist, sometimes you must purchase two complementary guides to a field or obtain alternatives. Nonetheless, it *is* possible for you to have a learning map of your own.

In the following pages, eight of the most useful research guides are described briefly. They vary in quality; put together, they illuminate the ideal.

Barzun, Jacques, and Henry F. Graff. *The Modern Researcher.* 3d ed. New York: Harcourt Brace Jovanovich, 1977. 378 pp.

The most widely useful guide of all. Both authors are well-known and respected historians. Their advice on research methods can be applied not just to work in history, but to work in all the social sciences and even in areas of the humanities and sciences. The book's chapters are essays, a few heavily bibliographic, but all informally, sometimes humorously, and gracefully written. About one-third of the book has to do with the nature of history or fact-finding in general, under headings such as "Historical Writing in Daily Life," "The Changing

Uses of a Changing Past," "The Searcher's Virtues." Here the advice overlaps with what a critical guide would say. Another third has to do with specific research practices, for instances, "Cross-Questioning the Book," "Disentanglement, or Undoing the Knots in Facts," "The Scholar and the Great Ideas." Most of the advice here concerns handling facts and ideas with integrity. This is the "training" portion of the book. Only a small segment has to do directly with the use of reference materials, and although that is excellent on basics, and although the book does include a bibliography of around 300 items, it does not claim to rival descriptive guides in history. The final third has to do with writing research papers; it provides the equal of what you might learn from many college composition texts. There is a subject, title and author index. No other guide contains as many, as detailed, and as wide-ranging examples of research problems as *The Modern Researcher*, and none examines the issues behind research as thoroughly. Few attempt to give advice on so many phases of research. None is as good on the subject of converting raw information and ideas into a convincing written work. Its publisher calls it a "classic" and it is.

Muehsam, Gerd. *Guide to Basic Information Sources in the Visual Arts*. Santa Barbara, Calif.: ABC-Clio, 1980. 289 pp.

One of the best examples of a critical guide to a particular field. Designed for art students and art history majors, it is divided into four parts, "Core Materials," "Periods of Western Art," "Art Form and Techniques," and "National Schools of Art." This organization, largely by subject, is especially suited for problem-solving. The chapters are bibliographic essays. Numerous headings such as "How to Get Information about Artists," and the author's writing style itself encourage a do-it-yourself approach. Basic instruction is provided—e.g. a review

of the catalogue card—and definitions of the most
common terms in art history are supplied. All these
features serve an introductory audience. Yet advanced researchers can profit from knowing, for example, that certain commonly used periodical bibliographies are available in computerized form. The
nonprint resources for studying art are treated with
the importance they demand. All in all, some 1045
publications are discussed, making the coverage
quite thorough for a critical guide. (Its descriptive
counterpart by Donald Ehresmann [see page 93],
which attempts to be comprehensive, has 1670 entries.) Cross-references are eased by a title, subject,
and author index. But what gives the greatest bene-
fit are Muehsam's evaluations as she describes
sources or strategies. Although she is a librarian,
she conveys an art historian's sense of what studying art is all about, what the traditions have been,
and what the possibilities are today. Moreover,
Muehsam teaches you about the resources for art
history without assuming that the value of such research is self-evident, and without getting caught
up in any single fashion of research.

Frantz, Charles. *The Student Anthropologist's Handbook: A Guide
to Research, Training and Career.* Cambridge, Mass.:
Schenkman, 1972. 228 pp.

Frantz, a professor, writes in an informal style.
This critical guide takes a uniquely practical approach to its field. The series of bibliographic essays begins with a chapter on what anthropology is,
its scope, history, characteristics, organization and
relevance. Two other chapters, "Becoming an Anthropologist" and "The Practising Professional,"
draw your attention in a commonsense way past
research toward a career. Next, chapters on field
and laboratory research and on anthropology's main
sources—people, libraries and museums—demon-
strate that research ranges far beyond work with

published material. Even certain ethical questions involved in research are touched upon. While all these practical matters are relevant to anthropology rather obviously, they are, of course, relevant to any other discipline as well, and critical guides do well to mention them. Frantz's conventional "guide to the literature" chapters (five subdivisions of anthropology plus "Culture Areas and Regional Studies") are competent, if limited. Unfortunately, there is no index.

Bottle, R. T., ed. *Use of Chemical Literature.* 3d ed. Woburn, Mass.: Butterworths, 1979. 306 pp.

This critical guide has about 20 chapters written in the form of bibliographic essays, with an index. As an example of an advanced guide for a single field, some chapters deal with general types of reference sources, others with chemistry's subfields. An Introduction and initial chapter on the use of libraries is good for users at any level, but in the other essays quite a bit of background knowledge is assumed. British materials are stressed. Certain matters of interest to introductory users, such as a rationale for research in chemistry, or guidance in chemistry as a career, are passed over. On the other hand, a chapter on the history and biography of chemistry is included and actually is an excellent capsule text; most science research guides ignore origins and personalities. There is also a chapter on the practical use of the chemical literature that fits introductory needs. As a bonus, exercises with answers are provided. Mainly, however, this guide has earned an excellent reputation because of its comprehensiveness combined with authoritative commentary. Although chemistry probably has more research guides than any other discipline, none covers as much as Bottle's and none contains as much evaluation-in-context for each reference tool. Even unconventional research methods are discussed.

Bottle's guide belongs to a series of critical guides that has achieved distinction, "Information Sources for Research and Development," published in England by Butterworths. All of its volumes are organized in the same general way. Although they are not all equally good, several of them have the same excellent qualities as *Use of Chemical Literature* and may be found on the supplemental list below.

Patterson, Margaret. *Literary Research Guide*. 2nd ed. New York: Modern Language Association, 1983. 559 pp.

Another example of an excellent guide for a particular field, though quite different from the three just discussed. Its format is that of a descriptive guide, and one of its strong points is its comprehensiveness: it covers about 1650 items. These items range widely, too, for they include works on certain aspects of English study that other guides do not (for instance, such practical aids as teaching and grant-getting resources), and a relatively large proportion concerns fields allied with English. The guide has certain features that differentiate it from most other descriptive guides, however, and offer you unusual access. A "regular" index includes names, titles, and subjects; also, a short-title table of contents serves as a second, more extensive subject index. In addition, there is a reference section especially devised to meet common problems, and quite a bit of basic instruction throughout on how to use a library. Finally, the bulk of the Introduction is a step-by-step guide to the analysis of questions that can facilitate the research procedure, whether simple or complex. In addition, *Literary Research Guide* contains longer and more distinctive annotations than most descriptive guides. Their length varies to match the entry's significance, and their style is informal. Besides providing the usual sort of evaluation, the entries try to illustrate the type of problem each work is designed to solve. The

quality of these annotations has been disputed, but it can assuredly be said that this guide assumes a more general audience than most other single-discipline descriptive guides, and it uses innovative methods to engage the least advanced segment of that audience while meeting the needs of more experienced users, as well.

Vose, Clement E. *A Guide to Library Sources in Political Science: American Government*. Washington, D.C.: American Political Science Assn., 1975. 136 pp.

This is extremely limited in coverage and has no index, but it does contain notably long and enlightening critical evaluations. It is written as a series of bibliographic essays. Some of its comparisons of particular titles are informed by the author's extensive and original research, for instance, those in the section on general reference works (almanacs, biographies, political dictionaries, and encyclopedias). This section, as well as the chapter on library basics, could profitably be read by learners at any level in any of the social sciences. The other chapters cover research on parts of American national government (government publications, the Constitution, Congress, the executive branch, federal courts) and archives. The author has teamed with reference librarians in his teaching of undergraduates, so the guide has especially constructive examples. It also differs from most other research guides in having illustrations (an illustrative chart is available too). More fundamentally, the author's longtime teaching experience has determined the guide's constant theme of "why." You are led to consider the purpose of what you are doing as a principal consideration in where to turn. This involves at least an implicit review of some of the major subfields within political science, and explicit reminders about the discipline's worst pitfalls. The guide also is admirably open-ended: "The aim in

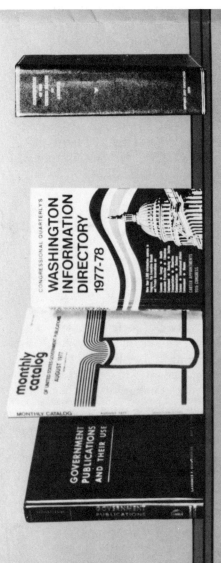

1 A detailed road map through the maze of information sources in the capital can be found in the *Washington Information Directory*. Arranged by subject, it contains more than 5,000 entries on Congress, the executive branch and private associations. Other features include listings of members of Congress and their key staff aides, congressional committees, foreign embassies, labor unions and regional offices of federal agencies. The directory is published annually by Congressional Quarterly Inc. The *Monthly Catalog of United States Government Publications* is the basic bibliography to government publications and is available from the Government Printing Office. The December issue contains the annual index. Explanations of fine points about the *Monthly Catalog* and other bibliographic keys are in Schmeckebier and Eastin's *Government Publications and Their Use*.

2 The Constitution vested all legislative powers in Congress. The powers of and constitutional limitations on Congress have been reviewed by the federal courts in thousands of cases. The most important rulings are summed up, under the appropriate clauses, in *The Constitution: Analysis and Interpretation* by the Congressional Research Service, Library of Congress.

these essays about how political scientists, young and old, might garner knowledge from libraries is to catch the reader's interest as a spur to further individual study. The try is to catch and stimulate curiosity, not to satiate it." (vii)

It is much harder to find good research guides covering interdisciplinary fields, for obvious reasons, than it is to find those covering the conventional ones. Below are two works that manage to do the job well, although both are longer than the other research guides reviewed here, and, interestingly, neither was primarily designed as a research guide.

Stineman, Esther. *Women's Studies: A Recommended Core Bibliography*. Littleton, Colo.: Libraries Unlimited, 1979. 670 pp.

Meant to tell librarians building a women's studies collection what books they should buy; yet you can use it as a research guide. It is comprehensive, listing almost 1,800 items. Also, it has lengthy annotations, often evaluative and considered authoritative. These are enhanced by brief scope notes at the beginning of each chapter to give you a broader perspective and suggestions for further study. Author, title and subject indexes make cross-referencing convenient for a variety of uses. Finally, Stineman is probably the most well-known of women's studies librarians, one of the pioneers in that field. All these points make the work an excellent descriptive guide.

Some unique features make it even more useful, however. For one, Stinemen includes in her annotations frank mention of whether a work is feminist or not, saying she doesn't want to sidestep controversy (12). While this approach risks suppressing, rather than supporting, research, Stineman manages on the whole to make her evaluations seem especially honest and research in general more serious. An-

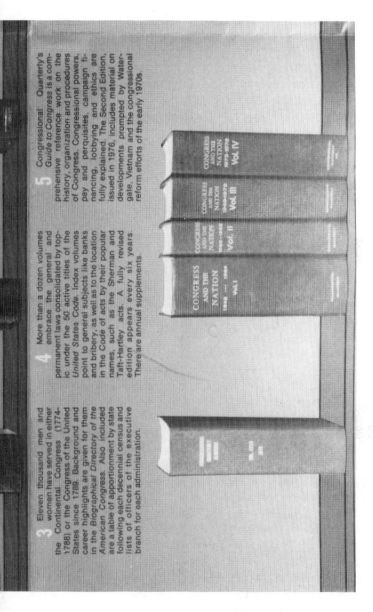

3 Eleven thousand men and women have served in either the Continental Congress (1774-1788) or the Congress of the United States since 1789. Background and career highlights are given for them in the *Biographical Directory of the American Congress*. Also included are a table of apportionment by state following each decennial census and lists of officers of the executive branch for each administration.

4 More than a dozen volumes embrace the general and permanent laws consolidated by topic under the 50 active titles of the *United States Code*. Index volumes point to general subjects like banks and bribery, as well as to the location in the Code of acts by their popular names, such as the Sherman and Taft-Hartley acts. A fully revised edition appears every six years. There are annual supplements.

5 Congressional Quarterly's *Guide to Congress* is a comprehensive reference work on the history, organization and procedures of Congress. Congressional powers, pay and perquisites, campaign financing, lobbying and ethics are fully explained. The Second Edition, issued in 1976, includes material on developments prompted by Watergate, Vietnam and the congressional reform efforts of the early 1970s.

Small segment of a wall chart, *Understanding Congress*. Copyright © 1980 by Congressional Quarterly Inc. Reproduced with permission.

other feature has to do with the guide's organization: though its chapters follow disciplines (e.g., anthropology, law, history), the scope notes, the attention to cross-referencing and the annotations themselves emphasize inter- or cross-disciplinary study. Last, Stineman's book incorporates more nontraditional materials than most research guides do. All of these procedures are in keeping with feminist ideals about and contributions to learning, or even to life.

Hammond, Kenneth A., George Macinko, and Wilma B. Fairchild, eds. *Sourcebook on the Environment: A Guide to the Literature.* Chicago: University of Chicago Press, 1978. 614 pp.

Initiated and designed by the Association of American Geographers as, in effect, a statement about geography's commitment to environmental education. The editors—two professors and a former journal editor—have all been involved with that cause in some way. The book contains four major sections: Environmental Perspectives and Prospects; Environmental Modification: Case Studies; Major Elements of the Environment (air, water, landforms and soils, vegetation, animals, coastal zones, human beings, energy); and Research Aids (environmental periodicals and organizations, and federal environmental legislation). Within each of the first three sections, an Introduction is followed by eight essays on particular topics, each written by an authority and drawn from a variety of disciplines. The last section, much briefer, comprises three sets of annotated lists. The essays outline the major subdivisions of the topic and cite the important sources for studying those, giving substantial bibliographies at the end. They cover reference tools far less than most research guides do; instead, they cover content directly. Also, of course, they are not uniform, and not much attention can be

paid in the text to cross-referencing, even though an author and subject index is provided. Yet all the essays are written for a broad audience, and that alone is useful, for one peculiarity of environmental study is that the experts and the general learners are so often so far apart in what they know. Moreover, the effort in this source book to be comprehensive is singular among guides to research in the environment. Not only technical but philosophical issues are explored, and the range of each is wide. Although this work is not a critical guide in the sense that term has been used throughout this section, it is the nearest thing to it, and can be respected for more than just its singularity.

The eight guides profiled hold particular interest, but others, too, are either excellent or uniquely useful. They are listed next, by field, alphabetically within each category.

The excellent ones are those that maintain a critical perspective on the research problems and resources for their field. They do so by what they say in their descriptions of the field or in their annotations. They can also express a critical perspective by drawing attention to a discipline's least bookish aspects: its non-library methods of research, its standards of scholarship or ethics, its associated professions, perhaps its politics. After inaccuracy, the worst failing of a research guide is to neglect broad questions about the purpose of research—to make comprehensiveness an end in itself.

Attention to the needs of researchers at a variety of levels is also excellent, as the general tendency is to overspecialize. Thorough and imaginative indexing helps with breadth. A wide net serves the needs not only of many researchers, but also of single ones, for considering how messy learning is, each person may be at a different level depending on different stages in the research process, or even depending on different sorts of research questions.

The guides that are uniquely useful—a couple of

the descriptive guides—appear because they are the only ones of their kind. This is a limited recommendation. Since no guide is ideal for all purposes, however, you should try using a title before you buy it. The list here is intended as a preliminary screening.

Photograph by D. C. Bell.

Humanities

GENERAL
Descriptive
Rogers, A. Robert. *The Humanities: A Selective Guide to Information Sources.* 2d ed. Littleton, Colo.: Libraries Unlimited, 1980. 355 pp.

ART
Critical
Jones, Lois S. *Art Research Methods and Resources: A Guide to Finding Art Information.* Dubuque, Iowa: Kendall/Hunt, 1978. 243 pp.
Descriptive
Ehresmann, Donald L. *Fine Arts: A Bibliographic Guide to Basic Reference Works, Histories and Handbooks.* 2d ed. Littleton, Colo.: Libraries Unlimited, 1979. 349 pp.

ENGLISH AND COMPARATIVE LITERATURE
Critical
Bateson, Frederick W., and Harrison T. Meserole. *A Guide to English and American Literature.* 3d ed. New York: Longman, 1976. 352 pp.
Gibaldi, Joseph, ed. *Introduction to Scholarship in Modern Languages and Literatures.* New York: Modern Language Association, 1981. 143 pp.
Descriptive
Altick, Richard, and Andrew Wright. *Selective Bibliography for the Study of English and American Literature.* 6th ed. New York: Macmillan, 1979. 180 pp.
Kehler, Dorothea. *Problems in Literary Research: A Guide to Selected Reference Works.* 2nd ed., rev. and enl. Metuchen, N.J.: Scarecrow, 1981. 196 pp. (With *Instructor's Index and Solutions to Research Problems.*)
Schweik, Robert C., and Dieter Riesner. *Reference Sources in English and American Literature: An Annotated Bibliography.* New York: Norton, 1977. 258 pp.
Training
Altick, Richard D. *The Art of Literary Research.* 2d ed. New York: Norton, 1975. 300 pp.

MUSIC
Critical
Watanabe, Ruth T. *Introduction to Music Research*. Englewood,
N.J.: Prentice-Hall, 1967. 237 pp.
Descriptive
Duckles, Vincent. *Music Reference and Research Materials: An
Annotated Bibliography*. 3d ed. New York: Free Press,
1974. 526 pp.

PHILOSOPHY
Critical
See articles on philosophical bibliographies, dictionaries, en-
cyclopedias and journals in *The Encyclopedia of Philosophy*,
Edwards, Paul, ed. New York: Macmillan and Free
Press, 1967. Vol. 6.
Descriptive
DeGeorge, Richard T. *The Philosopher's Guide to Sources, Re-
search Tools, Professional Life, and Related Fields*. Rev. ed.
Lawrence, Kans.: Univ. Press of Kansas, 1980. 220 pp.

RELIGION
Descriptive
Karpinski, Leszek M., comp. *The Religious Life of Man: Guide to
Basic Literature*. Metuchen, N.J.: Scarecrow, 1978. 399
pp.

THEATRE
Descriptive
Whalon, Marion K. *Performing Arts Research: A Guide to Infor-
mation Sources*. Detroit, Mich.: Gale, 1976. 280 pp.

Social Sciences

ECONOMICS
Critical
Fletcher, John, ed. *Use of Economics Literature*. Woburn, Mass.:
Butterworths, 1971. 310 pp.
Descriptive
Melnyk, Peter. *Economics: Bibliographic Guide to Reference Books*

and Information Sources. Littleton, Colo.: Libraries Unlimited, 1971. 263 pp.

HISTORY
Critical
Poulton, Helen J., and Marguerite S. Howland. *The Historian's Handbook: A Descriptive Guide to Reference Works.* Norman, Okla.: Univ. of Oklahoma Press, 1972. 300 pp.

POLITICAL SCIENCE
Critical
Kalvelage, Carl, Morley Segal, and Peter J. Anderson. *Research Guide for Undergraduates in Political Science.* 2d ed. Glenview, Ill.: Scott, Foresman, 1976. 140 pp.

PSYCHOLOGY
Critical
Sarbin, Theodore R., and William C. Coe. *The Student Psychologist's Handbook: A Guide to Sources.* Cambridge, Mass.: Schenkman, 1969.

SOCIOLOGY
Critical
Bart, Pauline, and Linda Frankel. *The Student Sociologist's Handbook.* 3d ed. Glenview, Ill.: Scott, Foresman, 1981.

WOMEN'S STUDIES
Descriptive
Oakes, Elizabeth H., and Kathleen E. Sheldon. *Guide to Social Science Resources in Women's Studies.* Santa Barbara, Calif.: ABC-Clio, 1978. 162 pp.
Schlacter, Gail A., and Donna Belli. *Minorities and Women: A Guide to Reference Literature in the Social Sciences.* Los Angeles: Reference Services, 1977. 349 pp.

Sciences

GENERAL
Descriptive
Malinowsky, Harold R., and Jeanne M. Richardson. *Science*

and Engineering Literature: A Guide to Reference Sources. 3d ed. Littleton, Colo.: Libraries Unlimited, 1980. 342 pp.

ASTRONOMY
Descriptive
Seal, Robert A. *A Guide to the Literature of Astronomy.* Littleton, Colo.: Libraries Unlimited, 1977. 306 pp.

BIOLOGY
Critical
Bottle, R. T., and H. V. Wyatt, eds. *Use of Biological Literature.* 2d ed. Woburn, Mass.: Butterworths, 1972. 379 pp.
Smith, Roger C., W. Malcolm Reid, and Arlene E. Luchsinger. *Smith's Guide to the Literature of the Life Sciences.* 9th ed. Minneapolis: Burgess, 1980. 223 pp.

CHEMISTRY
Critical
Maizell, Robert E. *How to Find Chemical Information: A Guide for Practicing Chemists, Teachers and Students.* New York: John Wiley, 1979. 261 pp.
Descriptive
Antony, Arthur. *Guide to Basic Information Sources in Chemistry.* New York: Halsted, 1979. 219 pp.

GEOGRAPHY AND ENVIRONMENTAL SCIENCE
Critical
Brewer, J. Gordon. *The Literature of Geography: A Guide to Its Organization and Use.* 2d ed. Hamden, Conn.: Shoe String, 1978.
Durrenberger, Robert W. *Geographical Research and Writing.* New York: Thomas Y. Crowell, 1971. 246 pp.

GEOLOGY
Critical
Wood, D. N., ed. *Use of Earth Sciences Literature.* Woburn, Mass.: Butterworths, 1973. 459 pp.
Descriptive
Ward, Dederick C., Marjorie W. Wheeler, and Robert A. Bier, Jr. *Geologic Reference Sources.* 2d ed. Metuchen, N.J.: Scarecrow, 1981. 590 pp.

MATHEMATICS
(not including Computer Science)
Critical
Dorling, A. R., ed. *Use of Mathematics Literature*. Woburn, Mass.: Butterworths, 1977. 260 pp.
Schaefer, Barbara K. *Using the Mathematical Literature: A Practical Guide*. New York: Marcel Dekker, 1979. 141 pp.
Descriptive
Dick, Elie M. *Current Information Sources in Mathematics: An Annotated Guide to Books and Periodicals, 1960–72*. Littleton, Colo.: Libraries Unlimited, 1973. 281 pp.

PHYSICS
Critical
Coblans, Herbert, ed. *Use of Physics Literature*. Woburn, Mass.: Butterworths, 1975. 290 pp.

Sample Questions for Research Guides

1. How can I find out if Bess Truman is still living?

2. My psychology professor says I should graduate from *Readers' Guide.* What's wrong with *Readers' Guide?* What should I graduate to?

3. I want to know if I can browse through the stacks to get ideas for my religion paper. How are the books on religion arranged?

4. Where can I get a handbook of specialized terms in biology?

5. I need to use some government documents for my political science paper. They're not catalogued in the regular way, I know, and they're kept in a separate part of the library. How should I start?

6. Is the *Encyclopedia of the Social Sciences* the same as the *International Encyclopedia of the Social Sciences?* Which is better?

7. I keep hearing that philosophy is dead. Do philosophers nowadays just study the past? What are the main fields of philosophy anyway?

8. My physics paper is about Mme. Curie. Does any library in this country have an extensive collection on her?

9. Can I find a reference work anywhere that lists the most significant scholarly work published last year on Robert Frost and briefly reviews it?

10. What guidelines should I use in judging whether the evidence presented in this book about Margaret Mead is authoritative?

Notes on Research Guides

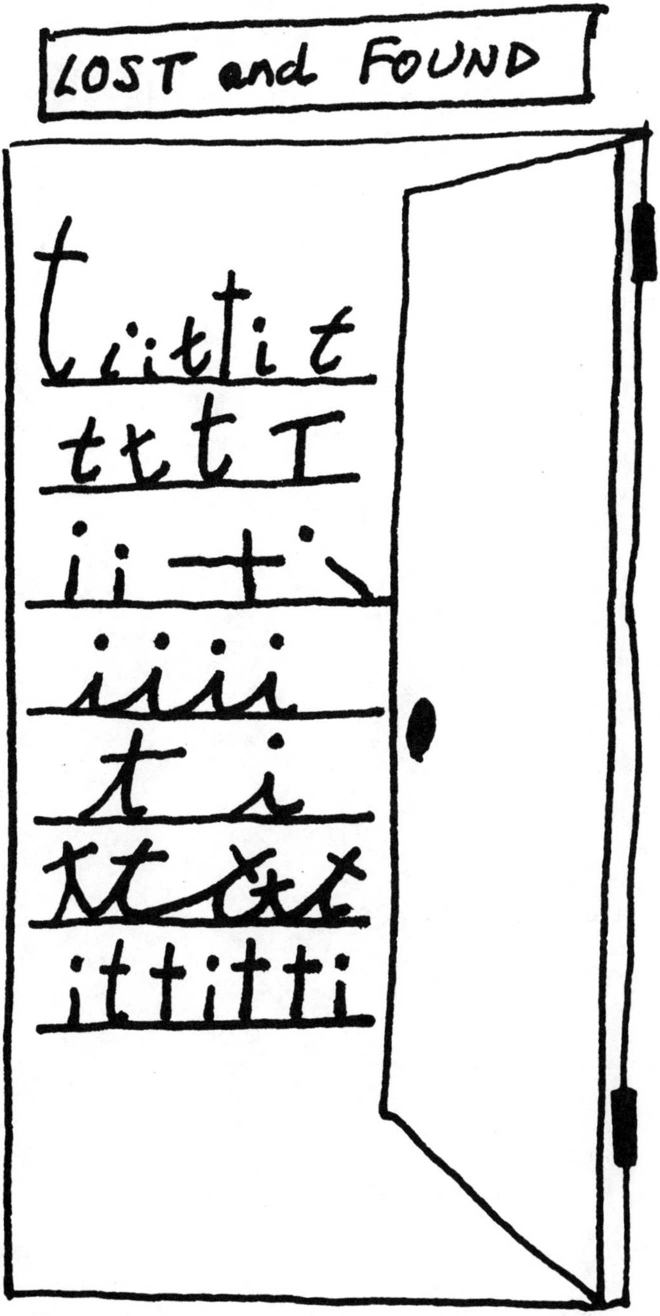
LOST and FOUND

6. STYLE MANUALS

Reading maketh a full man, conference a ready man, and writing an exact man.

Francis Bacon (1561–1626)

You are bound to write research papers several times during your learning career, and unless you can afford to hire an editor, not to mention a typist, you need to know the rules about manuscript preparation. You can find them in what is called, somewhat confusingly, a style manual. This is not a tool to teach you how to write stylishly; it simply tells you how to get the results of your research into acceptable form. The rules are arbitrary to some extent, but they are designed to facilitate clarity and consistency in your writing. If you take them seriously at first, in the end you will not have to think about them at all.

Most good college dictionaries include a brief, all-purpose section on style, but you cannot rely on that to take you far, because, generally speaking, style rules in academic fields are extremely detailed and even differ somewhat according to whether you are working in the humanities, the social sciences, or the sciences. Although you may find some of the information that you need in one of the standard college composition texts (see Chapter 3), watch out for the typical chapters on documentation. They most often tell you the rules that apply only in the humanities, and rarely give examples of other kinds. It would be easier if all fields adopted the same conventions, and some professional groups prod them to do

so, but the difficulty is as great as getting all the NATO countries to adopt the same weapons systems. To do any sustained
writing or reading in a field—for instance, after you have
begun a major—you need to pay attention to its specific style
requirements. Some universities and colleges put out their
own style manuals. For instance, the University of California
at Santa Barbara publishes a 14-page pamphlet entitled "Instructions for the Preparation and Submission of Theses and
Dissertations" that is available free of charge in the library.
You should find out if your institution, or perhaps department, has one of these and follow it as far as it goes: that will
probably never be as far as the general style manuals listed in
this chapter. In addition, you can use a research guide (see
Chapter 5) to lead you to the right style manual; some even
include basic information on style, themselves. The list that
follows takes you a more direct route to the most authoritative
sources of information on style. Professional fields such as
law, medicine and engineering are not covered; you can refer
to the related academic fields, look in the bibliography of one
of the general manuals, or consult Appendix I if you need
information on these. Manuals are listed in order of preference
in the "Recommended" category, by field after that, and alphabetically under "Other."

Recommended

The Chicago Manual of Style. 13th ed., rev. and exp. Chicago:
    University of Chicago Press, 1982. 738 pp.
Turabian, Kate L. *A Manual for Writers of Term Papers, Theses,
    and Dissertations*. 4th ed. Chicago: University of Chicago
    Press, 1973. 216 pp.
*MLA Handbook for Writers of Research Papers, Theses, and Disserta-
    tions*. New York: Modern Language Association, 1977.
    163 pp.

    These are all general-purpose manuals. *The Chicago Manual*
is the "Bible" for most of the scholarly publishing community.
Regarded as authoritative in all editions since the first in 1906,

it provides the most detailed possible information on all phases of manuscript preparation and documentation, with attention to the greatest number of fields. The newest edition brings it up to date admirably. Its rules are accepted as standards for all subjects in the social sciences, and some of the sciences follow it as well. Unlike most other style manuals, it has impressive sales figures.

Of course, *The Chicago Manual* covers subjects that many students do not need to know, and while that is not a point against it, since it makes the manual impossible to outgrow, *A Manual for Writers*—popularly known as "Turabian"—abridges *The Chicago Manual* to a size adequate for typical undergraduate purposes. Turabian is frequently recommended by teachers in the social sciences (be careful not to confuse it with the same author's *Student's Guide for Writing College Papers*, listed in this chapter) and it will serve you well. It has just become outdated, however, since it is based on the 12th edition of *The Chicago Manual*; it is not as permissive as the new *Chicago Manual* and it may leave your most detailed questions unanswered.

The *MLA Handbook*, published by the Modern Language Association, sets the standard style rules for the arts and the humanities, generally speaking. Its rules differ significantly from those in *The Chicago Manual*, although it makes no claims to rival *The Chicago Manual* because it covers so much less. Recently an MLA committee recommended changes in the mechanics of documentation that would bring the two manuals closer together. Presumably, these changes will be reflected in later editions of the *MLA Handbook*; until then, if you have a joint major in, say, sociology and French, you will have to buy two manuals instead of one.

The leading professional organizations in some disciplines publish their own style manuals either to replace or to supplement the generally approved manuals mentioned thus far. In a couple of cases, the style sheet of the leading journal in the discipline is recommended as standard, and there are a few other cases of official disciplinary sanction in matters of style. All of these are listed below. Most of the publications are merely pamphlets, and some are even shorter. Although their

Photograph by D. C. Bell.

titles suggest that they are only meant for professors, they are useful for any writer of papers in the discipline.

ART

"Notes for Contributors," *Art Bulletin*. New York: College Art Association, [n.d.].1 p.

> Brief specifications under the headings of Manuscript Form, Bibliography and Footnotes, Illustrations, Book Reviews, Letters to the Editor, and Monographs. Can be obtained from the Association at 149 Madison Ave., NYC 10016.

BIOLOGY

Council of Biology Editors (CBE) Style Manual: a guide for authors, editors, and publishers in the biological sciences. 4th ed. Bethesda, Md.: Council of Biology Editors, Inc., 1978. 265 pp.

> Stylistic standards accepted by journals in all subfields of biology, and also by most science book publishers. More than a list of specifications, it discusses wider subjects such as effective writing and the use of statistics.

CHEMISTRY

Handbook for authors of papers in American Chemical Society publications. 3d ed. Washington, D.C.: American Chemical Society, 1978. 122 pp.

Specifications for journal articles in chemistry, including the abstract. Also useful for its descriptions of the journals published by the Society.

MATHEMATICS

Manual for authors of mathematical papers. 4th ed., reprinted with corrections. Providence, R.I.: American Mathematical Society, 1980. 20 pp.

Provides not only specifications for papers in mathematics but also advice on how to improve writing and on how papers should look in printed form.

MUSIC

Irvine, Demar Buel. *Writing About Music: A Style Book for Reports and Theses.* Rev. enl. ed. Seattle: University of Washington Press, 1968. 220 pp.

Papers in music naturally raise special problems that this book addresses in detail.

PHYSICS

Style manual for guidance in the preparation of papers for journals. New York: American Institute of Physics, 1978. 56 pp.

Specifications for physics papers. Rules concerning mathematical expressions differ from those in the American Mathematical Society's manual. A new edition is forthcoming.

POLITICAL SCIENCE

Style Manual. Rev. ed. Washington, D.C.: U.S. Government Printing Office, 1973. 548 pp.

Comprehensive, detailed treatment of U.S. government printing and publishing specifications. Supplements the general style manuals listed above regarding government documents and government material in foreign languages. Since these materials have always been regarded separately from other resources for research, their treatment demands special attention. In most respects, however, this manual is for professionals, not learners, and it is hard to use.

PSYCHOLOGY

Publication manual of the American Psychological Association. 2d ed. Washington, D.C.: American Psychological Association, 1974. 136 pp.

Specifications for articles in psychology journals, but often recommended for social science research.

SOCIOLOGY

The style rules of the *American Sociological Review* can be obtained from that journal and are generally accepted as standard.

Other

Jordan, Lewis, ed. *The New York Times Manual of Style and Usage: A Desk Book of Guidelines for Writers and Editors.*

Rev. ed. New York: Quandrangle/New York Times Book Co., 1976. 231 pp.

Not a style manual in the sense used here, but a dictionary giving the definition, spelling, punctuation or capitalization advice for words and phrases commonly misused and questioned by journalists. Also includes basic grammatical information and a few encyclopedic items. Unsuited for academic purposes.

Turabian, Kate L. *Student's Guide for Writing College Papers.* 3rd ed., rev. and exp. Chicago: University of Chicago Press, 1976. 256 pp.

A hybrid writing guide, research guide, and style manual, this overlaps particularly with Turabian's *A Manual for Writers*, recommended earlier. Useful if you are able to buy only one book, but nowhere near as helpful as three.

Van Leunen, Mary-Claire. *A Handbook for Scholars.* New York: Knopf, 1978. 354 pp.

Especially good for those who wonder *why.* Meant to rationalize and simplify scholarly mechanics. Humorous and commonsensical, written more as a narrative than as a manual, it flouts the standard rules in a number of cases and is much more flexible overall. Also has bonuses such as an Appendix on "The Vita." However, it is not the accepted or approved source of information on style in any field, and so it can only be used to supplement another manual.

Words into Type. Based on studies by Marjorie E. Skillin, Robert M. Gay, and other authorities. 3rd ed. Englewood Cliffs, N.J.: Prentice-Hall, 1974. 585 pp.

Comparable to *The Chicago Manual*. Widely used by editors, and more production-oriented than *The Chicago Manual*, although it includes some sections on how to write well that its rival lacks. Not as authoritative for scholarly writings, however.

Sample Questions for Style Manuals

1. Can I cite references the same way in my chemistry term paper as in my art history paper?

2. What is the maximum number of lines I can quote in the regular body of my paper before I must indent the lines quoted and single-space them?

3. What is an appendix for?

4. In footnotes, is the date and place of publication sufficient information to include, or do I also have to name the publisher?

5. When a comma and quotation marks need to be used in succession, does the comma go inside or outside of the quotation marks?

6. Should the titles of poems be underlined or put in quotation marks?

7. In footnotes, does the author's last or first name come first?

8. Do all papers have to have separate title pages?

9. Should I try to separate, in my bibliography, the books I

relied on heavily for ideas from the books I only used for
minor pieces of evidence? If so, how?

10. What's the proper form for citing a computer program as
a reference?

Choices for My Desk

Photograph by Apple Computer Inc.

7. CALCULATORS AND COMPUTERS
by Winifred Asprey

If God had meant man to have a computer, He wouldn't have given him a brain. That's what I say.

Attributed to a nun by Peter McWilliams in *The Personal Computer Book*

So far, the tools discussed in this guide have been associated with reading or writing—learning calls for literacy. It also calls for numeracy. No matter what your interests as a learner are, you will not have mastered the trade until you are comfortable handling numbers.

The tools that help you with numbers naturally differ from the others in your kit. To begin with, they seem to manipulate information, not provide it. This distinction, however, gets shaky and shakier as you use the tool. An indisputable difference is that the array of quantitative tools available to you outnumbers the others tenfold. Another difference is that the quantitative tools change much more rapidly. The life of dictionaries, synonymies, writing guides, and the like can be measured in decades; by contrast, the hardware to help you handle numbers changes within a year or so, and the software within months. Even the respected companies in the business change, unlike the situation with publishers of, say, encyclopedias. Considering these differences, this guide cannot evaluate the quantitative tools as specifically as it does the others. It reviews the criteria you should use for choosing a

quantitative tool, but it does not apply these to particular machines or programs. Regular review sources become all the more important to consult, then, and so the sort of material that has been put into Appendix I for other sections of this guide will be included here in the text.

Calculators

Calculators abound on the shelves of department stores. Luckily, they come in all styles—fat, thin, rectangular, square, desk-top, hand-held, high- and low-priced, foreign and domestic—because a portable calculator of some sort is as useful and necessary to a learner as a ballpoint pen. Even the conservative NCTM (National Council for Teachers of Mathematics) endorses the judicious use of calculators in elementary and secondary school classrooms. If you are in college, you will find a calculator invaluable for any beginning course in a field where statistics are important (most of the natural and social sciences), and even for freshman composition, where you may have to figure out the length of a life or a period, measure features of syntax, or count rhythms or words. (Of course, you can also use a calculator for such typical collegiate but extracurricular jobs as computing what your roommates owe on the telephone bill, determining what grade you must get on your geology paper to make a 3.0 average, or dividing a restaurant tip with your friends.)

A novice or nonscientist will find that the cheaper calculators (under $10) suffice. They provide keys for addition, subtraction, multiplication and division, with several displaying answers to eight decimal digits of accuracy. Many of them also have square root and percentage keys. (I cannot think of any reason why a general user would ever want to calculate a square root. Percentages, yes; I am puzzled, however, when friends call me to ask what numbers should be entered, and in what order, to find a desired percentage. For some reason, it never occurs to them to test the process on a known result. For example, they could easily answer the questions for themselves by running the problem: what percent of 1000 is 500?) At any rate, some of the cheaper calculators even provide

limited storage capacity, the ability to keep an intermediate result available until needed later. Many, particularly the shirt pocket or credit card size calculators, boast an automatic shut-off after nothing has been entered for several minutes. Calculators on the market today are reliable, typically providing up to several hundred hours of use. Some can be refurbished with a new set of batteries, while others are disposable like a Bic lighter or pen.

As a novice, what model should you buy? Go to any store and try out several. Does the keyboard suit your finger size? Is the display easily read? What about the instruction book? Does it include any examples? Pick and choose; you certainly will get your money's worth no matter what brand you decide on. To select two examples at random, Sharp offers an eight-digit display calculator for less than $10 with all the trimmings mentioned above; Montgomery Ward has a Technico calculator the size of a credit card that is just as inexpensive. A savings and loan institution, gas company, or other business may give you a free calculator, perhaps embedded in a watch or pen, if you become their customer.

A calculator that has built-in keys to perform advanced mathematical and statistical functions will prove essential if you move beyond the novice stage in the natural sciences, mathematics, computer science, or the social sciences that require quantification. Of course, the price of these calculators varies directly with their abilities to perform sophisticated operations. Many are programmable. Since their introduction on the market less than a decade ago, prices have plummeted while capabilities have increased. What will happen to them as personal computers advance in popularity is an open question, but relatively low cost and portability are strong arguments in their favor.

Consumer Reports of September 1982 contains an excellent article entitled "Low-Cost Calculators" that rates more than 30 calculators, each under $15, in terms of price, size, weight, format, key feedback, key feel, memory, automatic shutoff, battery type, additional keys, and comments. The article clearly explains in layman's language what you should look for in order to find the low-cost calculator that best suits you. Most probably, as with its articles on other products, the

magazine will come back to calculators at regular intervals in the future.

Personal Computers

In selecting the computer as its "Man-of-the Year" for 1983, *Time* magazine reflects the burgeoning national mania for personal computers, epidemic in its growth, with no signs of levelling off. Almost overnight, it seems, affordable personal computers burst on the public scene, attracting young and old alike. Is there anybody who has not heard of Pac-Man? Computer arcades overflow with teenage devotees who play with the concentration of high-level research scientists, and at-home video games keep entire families entranced. As for their use in learning, computers have permeated more and more classrooms, and give promise of becoming lifelong companions. Computer illiteracy has virtually become a crime. Colleges and universities, aided by lush foundation grants, are jumping on the bandwagon to eliminate this dread threat. Already some institutions—Carnegie-Mellon, Clarkson, and Drexel, for example—have made provisions to supply all entering freshmen with their own computers, and one university (Case Western Reserve) is experimenting with "paperless" homework: students will do assignments on their own computers, transmit them to faculty member's departmental computers, and get them back, again by computer, with grades and comments.

Many voices have been raised over the hubbub of computer mania to express concern. No one has actually proven that computer-assisted learning systems teach students better and more cheaply than the regular classroom techniques; nor, on the other hand, has anyone had the vision to see how entirely new systems of learning could be devised to take full advantage of computers. In education, as in other areas of human life, neither fact-finding nor philosophy has kept pace with technology. All that is in the background, however, as you set out for college. How does this computer revolution (and it truly is that) affect you as you set out for college? Perhaps you already have your own "micro," most likely a Radio Shack

Photograph by D. C. Bell.

TRS-80 or an Apple-II, which you will bring to college as proudly as your older brothers and sisters once sported a type-writer. If you do not have your own terminal, however, don't panic. Rather, take time to assess the computer facilities available at the college(s) of your choice before you leap into a purchase. You will probably be better off waiting until you are on campus.

Much will depend on your interests. If you are a natural or social science major, manipulating numerical data in sophisticated ways, even graphically, will be your highest priority. If you are a nonscientist you may use a personal computer for any task from practicing the declensions of Latin nouns to indexing a set of poems to composing electronic music, but undoubtedly in humanistic fields word processing is the greatest boon a personal computer can offer. Does your college, like Dartmouth, for instance, have adequate terminals around the campus so that access is not a problem? If so, you will

probably be better off using the facilities provided and delay-
ing a purchase. On the other hand, if you have to wait until
3:00 a.m. to schedule a half-hour session on a terminal, a
microcomputer in your own room makes a good night's sleep
possible. Does your college permit you to tie in with its main
computer via a modem (telephone link)? Does it charge for this
service? What software (canned programs, computer languages, etc.) are available on a micro and could substantial
gains be realized by linking up to a large computer? What
print-out capabilities exist and of what quality?

If you decide to purchase a micro, which brand should you
select and with what peripheral equipment? Whatever time
you allot to analyzing your needs and to comparison shopping
will pay incalculable dividends. Visit local dealers and insist
on time to try out various models. Talk with the personnel in
charge of computer services at your college, to knowledgeable
professors, and to your turned-on classmates. Don't under-
estimate how much you will grow. The more you learn, and
the more you become familiar with your micro, the larger its
memory should be to serve your needs. Remember to investi-
gate the local availability of parts and the cost of repair services in case your micro malfunctions, as it inevitably will
from time to time.

Consulting a hardcover book to help you make the choice is
not much help. Like the hardware and software they review,
books on computing and computers at best make a splash and
are gone tomorrow. Hundreds of editions that I have acquired
in the past 15 years are museum pieces. On the other hand,
monthly journals of quality contain up-to-date articles on issues of concern to both new and experienced users; they compare performances of the products of different vendors and
evaluate often extravagant claims. Concentrate on reading
computer journals, the best source of current information. If
these periodicals (see the recommended list below) are not
available in your college's library, borrow issues from professors and friends. Subscribe to one and exchange issues with
a subscriber to another. If your college is in or near a large
city, become aware of the computer expositions, panels, and
symposia that are open to all interested persons and often

directly aimed at students. Furthermore, many colleges and universities have established student chapters of ACM (Association for Computing Machinery), the top national professional association, and have joined with regular ACM chapters in the area.

Finally, once you have decided that a personal computer is for you, don't delay your purchase because of reports that new developments are on the horizon and prices are bound to go down. While it is true, as I have already emphasized, that advances in technology are occurring at a dazzling speed, you could easily wait forever if you are not willing to accept the state-of-the-art. Remember color TV, new models of cars, stereos? Plunge, but intelligently, into this new world.

Journals

Creative Computing. P.O. Box 5214, Boulder, CO 80321. 12 issues, $24.97.
Byte. P.O. Box 590, Martinsville, NJ 08836. 12 issues, $19.
Personal Computing. P.O. Box 2941, Boulder, CO 80321. 12 issues, $11.97.
Computing Reviews

> The first three are all readable, timely, and sympathetic to the uses of personal computers for learners. The last, published several times a year, is expensive and not for beginners, but should be of value to serious students of computer science, who can use it in the library.

Paperbacks

McWilliams, Peter A. *The Personal Computer Book.* Los Angeles: Prelude Press, 1982. 300 pp.
_____. *The Word Processing Book.* Los Angeles: Prelude Press, 1982. 251 pp.

Both books are highly recommended. They are written especially for novices, but have value for experienced users as well. With restrained but welcome humor, they present the issues confronting a would-be purchaser of machines and printers. The author gives specific recommendations on vendors, availability, and performance. A main reason these books rival journals is that twice a year McWilliams publishes updates, available on request with stamped envelope from the author at Box 69773, Los Angeles, CA 90069. Both books may be ordered by a toll-free call to 800-421-1809, or 800-328-3890, ext. 6013. They may be ordered by mail from Prelude Press, 944 North Palm, Los Angeles, CA 90069 or Ballantine–Prelude Press, 201 East 50th St., New York, NY 10022. They are also sold in bookstores. The epigraph for this section may be found on p. 136 of *The Personal Computer Book*.

Sample Questions for Calculators and Computers

1. For a paper I'm writing on the large size of contemporary art works, how can I convert the measurements I made at museums from feet and inches to meters and centimeters?

2. How can I calculate the average length of the books in Milton's *Paradise Lost* and see how much each book deviates from that?

3. How can I do a chi-square test on the data from this poll of campus athletes I took for my sociology class?

4. Can I generate a graph showing what the most productive period of Mozart's life was?

5. My economics class is studying the stock market. Can I discover whether five particular energy stocks have followed the path of the Dow-Jones average in the last ten years or diverged from it?

6. I understand how to do my calculus problems, but how can I speed up solving them to get the assignment in on time?

7. I've got all the information for the bibliography on my classics paper. How can I turn some of the entries into footnote form?

8. Can I store the data from this week's astronomy lab as-

signment so that I can easily correlate it with next week's lab?

9. How can I test some optional patterns of color in a design I'm creating for a studio art class?

10. Can I analyze the prose rhythms in this passage from *Moby Dick* for echoes of rhythms from the King James version of the Bible?

8. HANDBOOKS FOR CREATIVE THINKING

Aha!

Anon.

You have a problem. You have a paper to write and you can't find any topic you'd care to work on for more than two minutes. Or you have a topic but you can't think of a fresh approach. Your body is stale and your mind is stalled. You find thinking no fun. In this sort of mood, you usually decide to take a break. That plan sometimes works, but you really need another option, one that doesn't so much divert you from thinking as helps you feel more relaxed about it. Books that can pull you out of this rut are certainly not standard reference books, since they do not purvey facts and figures about conventionally defined subject areas. They do, however, carry information about the thought processes of learning. With this sort of tool, you can look inward to improve your work at the trade.

Some handbooks for creative thinking deal only with mathematical problems. Others, such as self-therapy books and manuals for meditation, explicitly divorce themselves from academic learning. The books reviewed in this chapter, however, suggest techniques for helping you think creatively about all sorts of problems, including academic ones, even though the means may not be those traditionally associated with intellectualization.

Most of these books are written either by psychologists or

by professionals in schools of design. In either case, they include a heavy emphasis on the way the human mind receives
and orders its perceptions. The text often demands illustrations; the overall format tends to be unusual. Whether the
written sections are long or short, their tone is personal and
informal—often humorous.

Titles below are arranged alphabetically in each category.
The criteria for evaluating this type of tool are, necessarily,
much more subjective than for any other type. What is good is
what turns you on. A handbook for creative thinking will not
make you brilliant, but at least it should help you learn with a
spark.

Recommended

Adams, James L. *Conceptual Blockbusting.* 2d ed. San Francis-
    co, Calif.: W. H. Freeman, 1980. 160 pp.
McKim, Robert H. *Experiences in Visual Thinking.* Monterey,
    Calif.: Brooks/Cole, 1980. 250 pp.

Conceptual Blockbusting identifies blocks to your thinking,
much like hitches in golfers' putting, and suggests ways of
overcoming them. The blocks it deals with are perceptual,
cultural and environmental, emotional, intellectual and ex-
pressive; suggested remedies include encouraging certain useful conscious attitudes, freeing the unconscious, and developing alternate or nonverbal thinking patterns. Originally
sponsored by the Stanford Alumni Association, the book is
written for a general, college-educated audience and is full of
engaging, productive exercises of various kinds. You will find
among them an impossible-figure exercise to help you avoid
stereotyping, a group problem-solving exercise to show how
fear of embarrassment can stifle your creativity, a dot-joining
exercise to liberate you from delimiting problems too closely,
and cannibal and missionary exercises that prompt you to
switch from verbal to mathematical strategies for solution or
vice-versa. Whether hard or easy (the emphasis is less on
brain-teasing than on brain-tickling), these examples are always well explained, mostly illustrated, and often funny. You

can pick and choose those that interest you most. The author succeeds at being both sympathetic and comprehensive in his suggestions for creativity.

Experiences in Visual Thinking is more limited than *Conceptual Blockbusting* because it focuses on only one strategy for creativity: the visual one. (Its cover shows an enlargement of an eye.) Actually, the book's section on Seeing covers pattern-seeking and analytical seeing as well as the more conventionally visual topics of proportion and cues to form and space, and its section on Imagining covers not only visual recall but directed fantasy, foresight, and insight. Still, *Experiences in Visual Thinking* emphasizes (1) sharpening your perception, for instance, through exercises on describing common objects; (2) improving your ability to see images in action, for instance, through exercises in various types of projection; (3) heightening your pattern recognition, for instance, through gestalt exercises; and (4) applying your visual thinking to abstraction, for instance, through exercises in idea sketching or forming pattern languages. The author of *Conceptual Blockbusting* considers *Experiences in Visual Thinking* "outstanding" and has used some of it in his own text. If you are a person who feels more comfortable with pictures than with words you will like *Experiences in Visual Thinking* more than *Conceptual Blockbusting* and will not miss too much.

Fair

deBono, Edward. *New Think*. New York: Basic Books, 1968.
Gordon, William J. J. *Synectics: The Development of Creative Capacity*. New York: Macmillan, 1971.
Osborn, Alex F. *Applied Imagination*. 3rd rev. ed. New York: Scribner's, 1979. 417 pp.

These three are regarded as founding fathers of the applied creativity field. *New Think* is an extended argument for what its author calls "lateral" thinking. This is roughly the same as what *Conceptual Blockbusting* calls "creative conceptualization" or what *Experiences in Visual Thinking* calls "visual thinking." *New Think* seems more limited than the others, however, be-

An unusual 3-dimensional object called a Klein bottle, which can hold water despite the fact that its inside turns into its outside.

cause instead of using a wide variety of concrete examples from all parts of human experience, deBono depends largely on a few hypothetical and abstract examples that he constructs for the purposes of his argument. During about half of the book he works with a few diagrams of simple figures that he reduces, expands, or reshapes in order to make certain points about the way analytic thought processes work. In the second half, his suggestions for different approaches in thinking are good, but they add nothing to what you can find in *Conceptual Blockbusting* or *Experiences in Visual Thinking;* indeed, they are more general. *New Think* encourages you to practice creativity and outlines a theory and a method for doing so, but it does not give you as much and as varied raw material for practice as the recommended books do.

Synectics is often cited as a manual for creative thinking, and Synectics trainers have been invited to sessions sponsored by colleges, civic groups and the like to teach creativity. However, Gordon's advice is much more limited than that of the other authors reviewed here. First of all, he focuses almost exclusively on the method of analogy for stimulating new ideas. The book's explanation of analogy and its practical suggestions for developing analogies are excellent, but analogy is only one of several effective approaches to creativity. Then, the book is not designed for practice. It does not include exercises. Indeed, much of it tells about the history and theory of Synectics. To illustrate its general approach, it does provide a good many examples of problems that Gordon and early Synectics followers tackled: these satisfy your curiosity rather than stimulate your imagination, however. Another problem is that most of the examples come from business—inventing a product that will make $3 million, or a vapor-proof closure for space suits—and these do not serve learners very well. Overall, *Synectics* is not intended as a manual for creativity; rather, it is intended to promote the Synectics program—trainers, workshops and all. Beyond taking a few steps, you cannot "do-it-yourself" with *Synectics*.

First published in the '50s, *Applied Imagination* is the best known of these books. Its author had a successful advertising career, and capped his professional life by founding an organization to teach and promote creativity. The book is full of

advice about how to uncramp your mind and tips for thinking up new ideas. The examples tend to be from business, the arts, and family life, rather than academe, and are now dated; also the relatively long text is designed to be read through, not to be consulted on an instant, although there are exercises. The references at the end of each short chapter add up to a useful overview of early research on creativity. Many of Osborn's ideas provide the basics that the above-mentioned books expand, update, and convert imaginatively into their own versions. Osborn is unmatched in his faith that creativity can (literally) save the world.

Other

Anderson, Barry F. *The Complete Thinker*. Englewood Cliffs, N.J.: Prentice-Hall, 1980. 278 pp.

> Similar to *The Art of Clear Thinking* in its broad range, with only a third devoted to creativity, other sections on memory, reasoning, heuristics for avoiding complexity, and various kinds of decision-making. Emphasis on "tree" diagrams for thought processes. Less readable, more like a text, than *Art of Clear Thinking* (see below), although meant for a general audience and full of examples. Exercises with answers.

Flesch, Rudolf. *The Art of Clear Thinking*. New York: Barnes & Noble, 1973. 212 pp.

> Of broader range than the other books reviewed here, this work deals with the psychology of thought, classification, the importance of language in thought, logic and statistics in addition to creativity. Useful references. Full of lively examples and nitty-gritty advice, written for a general audience. No exercises.

Koberg, Don, and Jim Bagnall. *The Revised All New Universal*

Traveler: A Soft-Systems Guide to Creativity, Problem-Solving and the Process of Reaching Goals. Los Altos, Calif.: Kaufman, 1981. 128 pp.

Treats more general topics than creativity, as title indicates. The most "hip" in this group, with the travel metaphor pursued throughout and illustrated with old-time engravings of travellers. Lists largely replace text format. Definitely catchy, but not as comprehensive as the other two books, and not as easy to relate to academic learning.

Sample Questions for Creativity Handbooks

1. How can I get myself in the habit of making connections between material I am learning in different classes?

2. How can I convert the numerical information for this economics paper into a visual form?

3. How can I get in touch with my physical sensations so that I can write as concretely as my English professor says I should?

4. Is there any way I can use material from my dreams in my academic career?

5. What are some useful tricks for memorizing chemical formulas?

6. Would it be possible to diagram the history of communism?

7. How can my friends and I brainstorm the exam we have on Wednesday?

8. My philosophy professor says I imitate the existentialist philosophers' abstractions instead of explaining them. How can I bring all that stuff down to earth?

9. I underline practically everything I read in the textbooks,

and so I can't remember anything. How can I learn to tell what's important from what isn't?

10. How can I come up with some new and vivid way to explain what happens in the Krebs cycle?

"Money spent on the brain is never spent in vain."

INVESTING IN YOURSELF

Dig a well before you are thirsty.

Chinese proverb

Prices for the books listed in this guide have not been specified because they change so rapidly; instead, the number of pages in the books has been noted as a relative indicator. Basic tools often cost less than other kinds of books learners use, but, for a guide, a 1982 study in Great Britain showed that the average cost of a scholarly book was $28: that figure can only go higher here. Of course, the cost of a calculator or a personal computer is a separate matter. (One knowledgeable estimate is that a personal computer sufficient for a college student's use nowadays costs $2,000. The vice-provost for computing at the University of Washington, remembering that when he started school a slide rule cost about as much as 10 books, says that computers for students will be priced about right when the same ratio applies.) Let's just estimate for the moment that if you could walk into your local bookstore and buy the book portion of the recommended basic tool kit off the shelf, it would cost $200. This is probably beyond your budget for books. You can get the kit much more cheaply, however.

You'll have to order some of the tools anyway, so you might as well consider the alternatives to a regular bookstore. Ordering reference books through a book club or the book-buying service offered by other sorts of clubs can cut the price. For instance, if you get your dictionary or synonym book through Verbatim Book Club, a group for language-lovers (Essex, CT

06426-0668), you can get a 20% discount. Writer's Digest Book Club (9933 Alliance Rd., Cincinnati, Ohio 45242) offers books at up to 20% off. Alumnae/i may pay 10% less for books from their universities' presses. You don't have to belong to these groups yourself; you can get an order blank or catalogue through a friend, or copy one at a library that gets the organization's periodical. Some book warehousing companies send out discount catalogues every two weeks or so where you can find bargains. (Examples are; the Publishers Central Bureau 1 Champion Ave., Avenel, N.J. 07001, and Barnes & Noble, 126 Fifth Ave., NYC 10011.) You can also obtain used reference books through a library book sale, a classified ad, or a used book outlet. The Reference Book Center at 175 Fifth Ave., NYC 10010 (the Flatiron Building) offers a particularly large selection of used reference titles. Your professor may have an extra copy of a basic tool or can steer you to someone who does. If you work on it, you can probably cut costs to $120 or less.

You can think of these tools as capital investments. They are like plant and equipment to a manufacturer, since they enable you to produce knowledge, for your own or others' consumption. If you didn't think you were going to profit from this product in the long run, you probably wouldn't have taken up the learning trade, so you might as well be prepared to put in what's necessary. You may have to take out a loan to purchase good tools—that's justifiable—or make a case to interested relatives that they can pool gifts to contribute to your kit.

Don't try to save money by buying your basic tools in paperback. Occasionally, you cannot get hardcover, particularly in the category of research guides, but whenever possible, do. Hardcover books do not fall apart or discolor in a couple of years. Their layout is spacious and they lie flat, so you can read them and take notes in them comfortably. They are books which are meant to last for life. This guide has not indicated the availability of titles in paper unless absolutely necessary. In an ideal world for learning, paperback editions of basic tools wouldn't even be published.

At this point, some remarks are in order about those other books the learner has to buy: assigned texts. At $30–$50 per

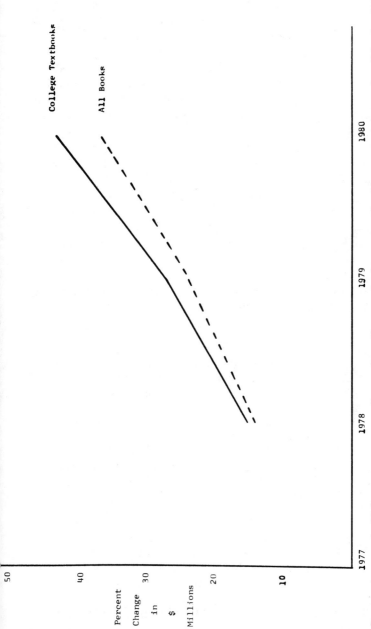

Percent increase in U.S. consumer expenditures for college textbooks compared with percent increase for all books, 1977–1980.
Source: *Bowker Annual*, Vols. 25–27.

course, you are probably spending more than is necessary on these. Start waiting a bit before you rush to the bookstore during the first few days of classes. Ask friends if you can take a look at their copies of the texts. The course may be one you're going to drop anyway. If not, see if you can get a used text. Try bartering for it. Don't neglect your relatives as a resource. Ask someone who knows more than you do about the subject, even the professor, to help you evaluate the text's importance for you. Look at one of the appropriate research guides mentioned in the previous section to see if it comments on the text. Quite possibly, you could substitute an edition in the library (and while you're at it, don't forget the public library as an alternative to the library at the institution where you're enrolled). Or the substitute could be a similar text that you already happen to own. A student of mine once wrote on his list of collegiate gripes that he had to buy "three copies of Plato's *Republic* [because of] professors who all insisted on *their* translation and pagination." This gripe shouldn't have to be as typical as it is.

You could even consider this suggestion from the *Next Whole Earth Catalog*, which may shake you up until you get rid of some popular misconceptions about the learning trade.

> If you're starting to learn about a field that you know nothing about, go to the children's library and get some fifth, sixth, seventh grade books about it before you go into grownup books. Basic books for grownups tend to be aimed at college freshmen taking required courses—and everybody knows that they're supposed to suffer, including the people who write the books. Basic books for kids are aimed at kids browsing in libraries who don't have to be there and could leave anytime. The books have colors and pictures and a will to sell the subject; the good ones assume you know nothing without being condescending. You can get some vocabulary and feel for the shape of the subject before you get into the stuck-up real books. Kids' books can also help you if you are one of those freshmen in one of those required courses.

The basic principle behind all these suggestions is that you

should not go out and buy assigned texts any less critically than you buy the basic tools recommended here. The basic tools will be more valuable to you in the long run, and a better alternative to getting them in paperback is to be more careful about what you spend for texts. In the end, when all your comparison shopping and tool hunting is done, remind yourself that whatever you have spent on your basic kit, like a good investment, will repay itself and then some.

Money-Saving Options

Library of Congress, main reading room.

CONCLUSION

They know enough who know how to learn.

Henry Adams (1838–1918)

If you were a learner in certain circles of medieval Europe, you would have needed only a single tool: the Bible. The Koran serves nowadays as the one-and-only, all-purpose learning tool for some groups in the Middle East. In our society, however, learning is not so simple. Call it liberal or merely modern, it stresses information over doctrine and so makes demands for tools on an entirely different scale. This guide has advised you about a minimum number of the most basic tools. These you should own. You will require many more, though, and for those you will need to use the library.

The library has all the tools that might have been included in this guide but were not. For instance, atlases and biographical dictionaries were omitted because they overlap with encyclopedias and dictionaries, while usage books overlap with encyclopedias. You can find titles of all these types, such as the *National Geographic Atlas of the World, Webster's Biographical Dictionary, Notable American Women, 1607–1950, Modern American Usage,* or *The Dictionary of the History of Ideas,* in the library. Almanacs, yearbooks, handbooks, and other such ready-reference tools were omitted because you have to buy new editions so frequently. You can find titles of these types, such as *Information Please Almanac, Facts on File Yearbook, Statistical Abstract of the United States,* or the *Guinness Book of World Records,* in the library. Books of quotations were omitted be-

cause they are less useful than a commonplace book (a collection of quotations or important points classified by subject)
that you keep on your own. You can find Bartlett's *Familiar
Quotations* in the library. A historian friend of mine believes a
local telephone directory, the IRS's instructions for preparing
your income tax, and *Robert's Rules of Order* are as basic to
learning as the tools listed here. You can find all three in the
library.

You can find plenty more, of course. You will come to
complicated tools—serial bibliographies, union lists, the *Science Citation Index*—that are indispensable for certain purposes
but that you don't need for most learning tasks and couldn't
afford anyway. To use tools like these, you must have special
instruction. Library orientation handouts, tours, and classes
coach you about them, as do the books suggested in Appendix
I. Whenever you hit trouble, however, run to a reference
librarian. You may be embarrassed to ask questions, but if
you have prepared by using your basic tools and if you have
tried working on your own for a while instead of making the
librarian's desk your first stop, then you needn't be embarrassed. One librarian I know is so helpful that he will tour the
shelves with students, picking out the best books for them to
use. Most reference librarians do not have enough time for
that, and probably should not be expected to do it. Nonetheless, many reference librarians say they are poorly utilized,
and one review of composition texts, which serve as most
learners' introduction to library research methods, shows that
"the texts reflect little understanding of the librarian's real
function and fail to recognize librarians as teachers."

Computers, of course, are changing access to information.
Experts project that libraries will become mostly automated
during the first quarter of the next century, and if you follow
the advice given in a preceding section on automated tools,
you may then be able to sit at home with your terminal and
never pass through another book detector again. You may
consult bibliographies, indexes, and other reference sources
on a screen instead of in printed volumes, and you may even
put together specialized sources from general ones on your
own. So why use the library? The mistake here is in thinking
that the computer will replace all other tools. It is a machine to

enable you to use the others more efficiently, but it cannot replace them. If you don't know how to use them in the first place, the computer will be of no help to you at all.

Perhaps you have heard a friend say something like the following, "I only have to work on that psych paper for a couple of days. My dad got his secretary to look up ten references for me so I don't have to go to the library, and then she'll type it for me when it's done." This cavalier approach to the library has inadvertently been supported by *A Nation at Risk*, from the National Commission on Excellence in Education, and other prestigious reports on learning. In their efforts to establish basic competencies, they consider the ability to use the library a "study skill," leaving it close to the end of their list of essentials. On the contrary, learning how to use the library is crucial to learning in general. The library is the ultimate supply house for tools, and, in our society, learning is a tool-intensive trade.

Once you have assembled your basic tools for learning and have the shelves of others arranged in your mind's eye, the next step in the trade, as an old cookbook instruction goes, is to "Face the stove."

> The best thing. . . [said Merlin the magician to his pupil Arthur], is to learn something. . . . Learn why the world wags and what wags it. That is the only thing which the mind can never exhaust, never alienate, never be tortured by, never fear or distrust, and never dream of regretting. Learning is the thing for you.

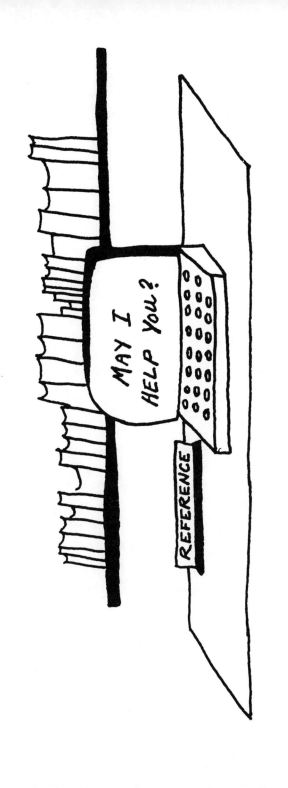

APPENDIX I

> *The only way in which one human being can properly attempt to influence another is to encourage him to think for himself.*
>
> Leslie Stephen (1832–1904)

To be true to its prodding toward self-sufficiency, this guide must make even itself expendable. Included below are the names of articles or books that will take you further in either considering each type of tool or evaluating specific titles. Each source has been helpful in the preparation of this guide, and a few have been quoted in the text, in which case the page reference has been noted.

Don't forget, as you think about each of the eight tools, that in many cases the front matter of a reference work itself is the best introduction to the type it exemplifies. In other words, READ THE DIRECTIONS.

Introduction

Brand, Stewart, ed. *The Next Whole Earth Catalog.* Sausalito, Calif.: Point, 1980. 608 pp.

> Access to tools is the theme of this work, and so a quotation from it is appropriate as an epigraph for *Tools in the Learning Trade.* Various headings in the *Catalog* feature learning tools that you might find

interesting, and you can look forward to surprises under the heading of "Learning."

Galin, Saul, and Peter Spielberg. *Reference Books: How to Select and Use Them*. New York: Random House, 1969. 312 pp.

Briefly describes and gives introductory directions for the use of about 200 reference works, many of them only appropriate for use in the library.

Gates, Jean Key. *Guide to the Use of Books and Libraries*. 4th ed. New York: McGraw-Hill, 1979. 275 pp.

Portion entitled "General Reference Sources" is similar to Katz's *Basic Information Sources (see* below), but much shorter and designed for undergraduates.

Katz, William A. *Introduction to Reference Work*. 3rd ed. 2 vols. New York: McGraw-Hill, 1978.

A standard text for reference librarianship. Vol. 1, *Basic Information Sources* [367 pp.], is designed for general readers as well. It discusses the value of reference sources overall, describes seven basic types, gives criteria for their evaluation, and comments on sample titles within each type. Katz's detailed and wide knowledge of information sources combines with a readable style to make this a good teaching tool. He also gives annotated suggestions for further reading at the end of each chapter. This work is the contemporary replacement for such classics as Louis Shore's *Basic Reference Sources* (1954), Robert Murphey's *How and Where to Look It Up* (1958), and Frances Cheney's *Fundamental Reference Sources* (1971).

Sheehy, Eugene P., ed. *Guide to Reference Books*. 9th ed. Chicago: American Library Association, 1976. 1015 pp. *Supplement*, 1980. 305 pp. *Second Supplement*, 1982. 243 pp.

The best-known reference titles often get called by the name of their editor, or, in this case, a succession of editors over the years. "Sheehy" is a comprehensive, classified, and annotated bibliography of reference works, regarded as one of the two most authoritative in publication. It is updated regularly. All the types of tools covered in this guide, except for the quantitative tools and the handbooks for creative thinking, are covered in Sheehy, and most of the titles can be found there too, although under varied headings. One section gives criteria for evaluating reference sources (*see* Appendix II). The only problem is that, even with special efforts, it is hard to keep current.

Taylor, Margaret. *Basic Reference Sources: A Self-Study Manual.* Metuchen, N.J.: Scarecrow, 1973.

A workbook for anyone who wants to get right to the shelves.

Walford, A. J. *Guide to Reference Material.* 3 vols. Vol. 1, 4th ed.; Vols. 2 and 3, 3rd ed. London: The Library Association, 1980, 1975, and 1977 for the volumes respectively. 2054 pp.

The other authoritative bibliography of reference works, along with Sheehy (*see* above). "Walford" emphasizes British materials, contains about 20 percent more entries than Sheehy, and is arranged with Vol. 1 covering science and technology; Vol. 2, the social and historical sciences, philosophy and religion; and Vol. 3, generalia, language and literature, and the arts. Otherwise, the same general comments that apply to Sheehy apply here.

Wyner, Bohdan S., ed. *American Reference Books Annual.* Littleton, Colo.: Libraries Unlimited, 1970–   , annual.

Reviews a wide selection of reference books each

year. Reference reviews may also be found in other periodicals, of course, but few devote themselves to this job entirely, as *ARBA* does. For mention of other review sources, *see* Gates or Katz (above).

Dictionaries

Hayakawa, S. I. *Language in Thought and Action*. 4th ed. New York: Harcourt Brace Jovanovich, 1978. 318 pp.

Not a book about dictionaries, but a standard and readable college text about the nature of language. Certain portions provide an excellent introduction to the problems of definition.

Katz, William A. *Basic Information Sources*.

Annotated in Appendix above under "Introduction." Has a section on dictionaries.

Kister, Kenneth. *Dictionary Buying Guide*. New York: Bowker, 1977. 358 pp.

Provides complete publication information on a comprehensive list of dictionaries and other word books—at all levels, for a variety of audiences—and comparatively evaluates each. Valuable and unique. Starts with a fine essay on the general points to keep in mind when choosing a dictionary. The only trouble is that it needs updating.

Murray, K. M. Elisabeth. *Caught in the Web of Words*. New Haven: Yale University Press, 1977. 386 pp.

The biography of James A. H. Murray (1837–1915), editor of the *Oxford English Dictionary*, this book teaches you about dictionary-using by drawing you into the spirit of dictionary-making.

Read, Allen Walker. "Dictionary" entry in *The New En-cyclopaedia Britannica*. 15th ed. 30 vols. Chicago: En-cyclopaedia Britannica, 1974. *Macropaedia*, Vol. 5, 713–22.

> A fine historical summary and introduction to general principles. The two quotations in the para-graph on usage level come from this article, pp. 715 and 716 respectively.

NOTE: Most writing guides (*see* section in text above) contain chapters on the dictionary that cover the basic points of how to use this tool.

Synonym Books

Katz, William A. *Basic Information Sources.*

> Annotated in Appendix above under "Introduc-tion." Devotes a short part of its section on diction-aries to books of synonyms and antonyms.

Kister, Kenneth. *Dictionary Buying Guide.*

> Annotated in Appendix above under "Diction-aries." Devotes part of its section on "Special-Pur-pose Dictionaries and Wordbooks" to books of syn-onyms and antonyms.

Webster's New Dictionary of Synonyms. (*See* publication informa-tion in text under "Synonym Books.")

> Its introductory essay is the best possible guide to the main types of synonymies and their uses.

Writing Guides

Burns, Shannon, et al. *An Annotated Bibliography of Texts on Writing Skills.* New York: Garland, 1976. 259 pp.

A classified bibliography that has more extensive
descriptive annotations than Trimmer's (below) and
about three times as many entries. Somewhat out-
dated, however.

College Composition and Communication.

Published quarterly by the National Council of
Teachers of English, *CCC* regularly reviews writing
texts and other books of interest to writing teachers
or users of reference books on writing. Occasionally
it devotes an entire issue to review articles.

Trimmer, Joseph. "Bibliography of Writing Textbooks,"
WPA (Writing Program Administration), 5 (Winter
1981), 31–48.

Classifies about 150 current writing texts and
provides one-or-two-sentence descriptive annotations.

One-Volume General Encyclopedias

Collison, Robert L. "Encyclopedia" entry in *The New En-
cyclopaedia Britannica.* 15th ed. 30 vols. Chicago: En-
cyclopaedia Britannica, 1974. *Macropaedia*, Vol. 6,
779–799.

Excellent background essay on encyclopedias in
general.

Katz, William A. *Basic Information Sources.*

Annotated in Appendix above under "Introduction." Has a section on encyclopedias.

Kister, Kenneth. *Encyclopedia Buying Guide.* 3rd ed. New York:
Bowker, 1981. 530 pp.

A companion to *Dictionary Buying Guide* (annotated in Appendix above under "Dictionaries"), and just as comprehensive and excellent overall in its comparative profiles. Its Introduction includes a fine discussion about the dim view many people take of encyclopedias. It has been updated more conscientiously than the *Dictionary Buying Guide*.

Research Guides

Sheehy, Eugene P., ed. *Guide to Reference Books*.

Annotated in Appendix above under "Introduction." Lists research guides under the heading of "Guides," by fields.

Walford, A. J. *Guide to Reference Material*.

Annotated in Appendix above under "Introduction." Lists research guides under heading of "Bibliographies," by field.

White, Carl M., et al. *Sources of Information in the Social Sciences*. 2nd ed. Chicago: American Library Association, 1973. 702 pp.

A work as comprehensive and well-respected as "Sheehy" and "Walford," only with a more restricted territory.

Style Manuals

The Chicago Manual of Style. (*See* publication information in text.)

Bibliography helpful, though not thorough, in

listing other style manuals. Certain of the others' stylistic practices are covered by *The Chicago Manual*'s text when especially technical cases arise.

Kister, Kenneth. *Dictionary Buying Guide.*

> Annotated in Appendix above under "Dictionaries." Includes a relatively short selection of style manuals in its section on books of "Usage and Idioms."

Sheehy, Eugene P., ed. *Guide to Reference Books.*

> Annotated in Appendix above under "Introduction." Includes style manuals under the headings of "General Reference Works, Bibliography, Printing and Publishing, Copy Preparation," and also under "Style Manuals," by field.

Walford, A. J. *Guide to Reference Material.*

> Annotated in the Appendix above under "Introduction." Includes style manuals under various headings, by field, but generally lists very few.

Handbooks for Creative Thinking

The best source of further information on creativity and creativity handbooks are the bibliographies of the books listed in the text. *Conceptual Blockbusting's* "Reader's Guide," relatively long and handy, is a bibliographical essay; the other books' lists are not annotated.

Investing in Yourself

Literary Market Place with Names and Numbers. New York: Bowker, annual.

You can find LMP on most reference librarians'
desks. It is full of all sorts of information on publishing that can help you with costs, including a list
of book clubs.

The Next Whole Earth Catalog.

Annotated in Appendix above under "Introduction." Keeps you in a cost-cutting spirit and gives
plenty of suggestions about how to translate that
spirit into action. The passage from the *Catalog*
quoted in this chapter is on p. 563.

Conclusion

Gates, Jean Key. *Guide to the Use of Books and Libraries.*

Annotated in Appendix above under "Introduction." Portions cover history of libraries, library arrangement, and library search strategies, in a readable, introductory vein.

Hartner, Elizabeth P. *An Introduction to Automated Literature
Searching.* New York: Marcel Dekker, 1981. 146 pp.

Rather technical for an introduction, but, sur-
prisingly, not many books of this sort are available.

Katz, William A. *Your Library.* New York: Holt, Rinehart &
Winston, 1979. 253 pp.

Not the equal of *Basic Information Sources* (*see* in
Appendix above under "Introduction") but nonetheless problem-oriented, readable, and reasonably
up-to-date.

Tiefel, Virginia. "Libraries and Librarians as Depicted in

Freshman English Textbooks," *College English*, 44 (September 1982), 494–505.

Title sounds specialized, but article actually includes readable and practical advice about how to use your reference librarian. The passage quoted in the Conclusion about composition texts' poor understanding of librarians is from this article, p. 500.

Todd, Alden. *Finding Facts Fast*. Berkeley, Calif.: Ten Speed Press, 1979.

Aimed more toward the typical information needs of reporters or free-lance writers than the needs of learners in academic fields, but worth consulting because of its emphasis on speed, its readable style, and a few pieces of sound advice that can be found nowhere else.

White, T. H. *The Once and Future King*. New York: G. P. Putnam's Sons, 1958.

A novel with an uplifting emphasis on learning. A passage from pp. 185–86 on the appeal of learning is quoted at the very end of the text.

NOTE: Composition handbooks all have sections on library research, but they are generally much less helpful than the books listed in this Appendix. Critical research guides provide good instruction about using the library; the only difference between them and the books in the Appendix is that the research guides are restricted to a special field. Some books with titles such as *The Research Paper: Form and Content*, *Writing and Researching Term Papers and Reports*, and *Student's Guide for Writing College Papers* seem to offer what you need, but they actually devote as much time to advice about writing as to advice about research, and so fall short of a composition handbook, on the one hand, and a research guide, on the other..(These books also

contain advice about how to use a few of the basic tools covered by this guide, but it is generally much too brief.) Elementary research guides—workbooks and skills tests—have also been written for some fields. Notable examples are the Pierian Press library research guides to biology, religion, history and sociology.

APPENDIX II

The following pages are reprinted from Eugene P. Sheehy, ed., *Guide to Reference Books*, 9th ed. (Chicago: American Library Assn., 1976), pp. xiv-xv. (*See* annotation in Appendix I under "Introduction.") In context, the material is intended to be read by reference librarians, but any college student should find it useful. It gives systematic advice about how to assess reference books, some of which has formed the basis for what is in this guide. It is reprinted by permission of the American Library Association.

Reference Books

However varied the work of a reference department may be, the reference book is the basis of its work. The most important element in the equipment of such a department is an adequate and live collection of reference books, and the most important asset of a reference assistant is a knowledge of reference books and experience in using the right book at the right time and in the right way. The possession of the right books and the knowledge of how to use them are two things essential to the success of a reference department, and the latter is no less important than the former. The ignorant assistant can render comparatively useless the finest collection of reference books, while the skilled assistant, who knows how to get from each book all the varied kinds of information that it is planned to give, can show astonishing results even when limited to only a few basic books.

From the point of view of use, books may be divided into two groups: those which are meant to be read through for

either information or enjoyment, and those which are meant
to be consulted or referred to for some definite piece of information. Books of this second class are called reference books,
and are usually comprehensive in scope, condensed in treatment, and arranged on some special plan to facilitate the ready
and accurate finding of information. This special arrangement
may be alphabetical, as in the case of most dictionaries or
encyclopedias; chronological, as in historical outlines and similar compends; tabular, as in the case of statistical abstracts;
regional, as in atlases; classified or systematic, as in the case of
some bibliographies, technical handbooks, etc. As such books
are used for the finding of single definite facts, some alphabetical approach to the fact is usually needed, and if the book
is not itself arranged alphabetically, it is usually provided with
a detailed alphabetical index. Works which follow any of these
indicated arrangements are reference books, pure and simple,
and are not used for consecutive reading.

There are other books, however, which, while intended
primarily to be read through for either information or plea-
sure, are so comprehensive and accurate in their treatment and
so well provided with indexes that they serve also as reference
books. Examples of such books are the *Cambridge History of
American Literature*, anthologies such as Stevenson's *Home Book
of Verse*, standard histories such as the *Cambridge Modern History*, and many of the textbooks and treatises used in college
work. The reference department of a large library will necessarily contain both formal reference books and these "border-
land" books as well, but the student of reference books will
naturally devote most of his attention to the formal reference
books, both because they are fundamental and because they
need careful study before all their uses can be learned. Later,
however, in doing actual reference work, he should realize
that the formal reference books constitute only a part, though
a very important one, of his collection of reference material
and that the treatment of some reference questions will in-
volve first the use of some standard reference book in the
reference collection, then reference from that to some book in
the stack to which the formal reference book has furnished a
clue, or even to some source of information outside the
library.

How to Study Reference Books

Only constant and practical use of a reference book will make a student thoroughly familiar with its character and use, but the following suggestions will help him in his preliminary examination of the book.

1. Examine title page carefully for information as to
   a) scope of work as indicated in title
   b) author's name
   c) author's previous record (often indicated by list of degrees, positions, titles of earlier works, etc.)
   d) publisher
   e) date of publication. Check date of publication by reference to copyright date and date of Preface; while these dates offer no absolute guarantee of the date of information in the book, they sometimes help in determining this especially in cases where they are considerably earlier than the imprint date.
2. Read Preface or Introduction for
   a) further information as to scope of work
   b) special features claimed
   c) limitations, if any
   d) comparison with other books on same subject
3. Examine book itself for
   a) arrangement
   b) kind of entry
   c) cross-references, i.e., extent to which included, whether given in main work or in separate list, etc.
   d) supplementary lists, noting number and kind and how connected with main work
   e) indexes, noting fullness and exactness of reference
   f) quality and kind of articles, noting whether they are popular or scientific, signed or unsigned,

impartial or biased, and especially whether they are equipped with satisfactory bibliographical references in the form of either appended bibliographies, references throughout the text, or bibliographical footnotes. Several articles should be read carefully, compared with similar articles in other books. The student should, if possible, look up some subjects upon which he has either some special knowledge or means of securing accurate information. However important the form and convenience of arrangement of a reference book may be, the trustworthiness of its information is of still greater importance and a knowledge of its comparative accuracy or inaccuracy is fundamental to any real knowledge of the book.

4. In examining both Preface and articles, note any evidence of lack of impartiality; e.g., if the book deals with a controversial subject, religious, political, etc., does it represent only one side; or, in the case of a biographical work, are the selection of names, kind and length of article, etc., determined in any way by the desire to secure subscribers.

5. In studying the arrangement of a book, note the possibility of variation in books which follow the same general arrangement; e.g., in a work arranged alphabetically, note what rules for alphabetizing have been followed. Among encyclopedias, for example, the *Britannica* and the *Americana* follow different rules, and the student who does not observe that fact may miss the article for which he is looking. The alphabetizing of words containing an umlauted vowel is a possible source of confusion in many books, and in foreign reference books, in general, one should always remember points in which the foreign alphabetizing differs from the English. A fuller discussion of some of these points will be found on page [102] of this *Guide*.

6. If the work in question purports to be a new edition, note carefully the extent of revision claimed for it and check this by comparison with earlier editions. New or revised editions often present very special difficulties, and the exam-

ination should be extended enough to determine whether
the revision is:

  a) so complete and thorough that it supersedes the
     earlier work
  b) thorough, but with the omission of some mate-
     rial included in the earlier work which is still
     useful, in which case the two editions may
     have to be used together, or
  c) so insufficient and superficial that the earlier edi-
     tion is still to be preferred.

A reference worker needs such information about a book
for two purposes:

  a) to decide whether or not the book should be
     purchased
  b) to be able to explain to readers who ask for a so-
     called new edition why its purchase was con-
     sidered advisable.

INDEX

About the Author and Contributor

BARBARA CURRIER BELL, an independent scholar, has taught writing and methods of research as a faculty member in the English Department and the College of Science in Society at Wesleyan University, and at Vassar College. Her Ph.D. is from Columbia University, 1972. Currently an officer of the Center for Independent Study in New Haven, Connecticut, she has written articles on literature, on reference tools, and on broader subjects in the humanities for a variety of professional journals, as well as publications with more general audiences. She has also held positions in educational administration.

WINIFRED A. ASPREY, a professor emeritus of mathematics and computer science at Vassar College, has had a long and distinguished career teaching undergraduates. She received her Ph.D. at the University of Iowa and taught mathematics at secondary schools before going to Vassar in 1945. Concurrent with her teaching, she has held numerous outside fellowship appointments, has been active in professional associations, and has directed the Vassar Computer Center.